INSTRUMENTAL

'*Instrumental* is no "misery memoir" . . . I have rarely read so cogent an account of the nature of victimhood . . . Visceral and palpable . . . Among the most powerful pages I've read all year'
SCOTLAND ON SUNDAY

'A life worth telling' *SPECTATOR*

'We're locked inside his head for long periods and it's a manic place to be. But he is brilliant . . . and insightful . . . James Rhodes writes at full volume' BLAKE MORRISON, *GUARDIAN*

'Bravo to a survivor who refused to be silenced . . . what really marks this book out is his confrontation with the unsaid (or rarely said) aspects of child sexual abuse and mental illness . . . Some of these thoughts verge on the taboo and it takes clarity, courage and intelligence to say them as plainly and honestly as Rhodes does'
INDEPENDENT

'I don't think I have ever read a more honest memoir than *Instrumental* . . . it is profoundly moving and deeply shocking. The truth is, it hits you like a slap in the face . . . What Rhodes has written is tough to take, at moments it left me reeling, and it demands utmost respect . . . I've never read anything quite like *Instrumental*'
SCOTSMAN

JAMES RHODES

A MEMOIR OF MADNESS, MEDICATION AND MUSIC

INSTRUMENTAL

CANONGATE

Edinburgh · London

First published in Great Britain in 2015 by Canongate Books Ltd,
14 High Street, Edinburgh EH1 1TE

www.canongate.tv

5

Quote from 'A Poet's Advice to Children' from *E. E. Cummings, a Miscellany*,
edited by George James Firmage. Published by Liveright Publishing Corporation.

Quote from 'After War, a Failure of Imagination' by Phil Klay © 2014,
Phil Klay and *The New York Times*.

British Library Cataloguing-in-Publication Data
A catalogue record for this book is available on
request from the British Library

ISBN 978 1 78211 339 3

Typeset in Bembo STD by Palimpsest Book Production Ltd,
Falkirk, Stirlingshire

Printed and bound in Great Britain by Clays Ltd, St Ives plc

MIX
Paper from
responsible sources
FSC® C018072
FSC
www.fsc.org

For my son

'If we fetishise trauma as incommunicable then survivors are trapped — unable to feel truly known . . . You don't honour someone by telling them, "I can never imagine what you've been through." Instead, listen to their story and try to imagine being in it, no matter how hard or uncomfortable that feels.'

– Phil Klay, veteran, US Marine Corps

CONTENTS

All of these pieces of music are available to listen to for free at
http://bit.do/instrumental

PRELUDE

CLASSICAL MUSIC MAKES ME HARD.

I know that's not a hugely promising opening sentence for some people. But if you scratch the word 'classical', perhaps it's not quite so bad. Maybe it even becomes understandable. Because now, with the word 'music', we have something universal, something exciting, something intangible and immortal.

You and I are instantly connected through music. I listen to music. You listen to music. Music has infiltrated and influenced our lives as much as nature, literature, art, sport, religion, philosophy and television. It is the great unifier, the drug of choice for teenagers around the world. It provides solace, wisdom, hope and warmth and has done so for thousands of years. It is medicine for the soul. There are eighty-eight keys on a piano and within that, an entire universe.

And yet . . .

My job description is 'concert pianist', and so there is, inevitably, a lot written about classical music in this book. It wouldn't surprise me in the least if some of the press around its launch will try as hard as possible to ignore that fact. They'll do that because core classical music doesn't sell anything, ever, and is seen by many as utterly irrelevant. And because everything about classical music, from the musicians themselves to the presentation of its product, the record labels, management – the whole industry ethos and ethics surrounding it – is almost totally devoid of any redeeming qualities.

But the unassailable fact is that music has, quite literally, saved my life and, I believe, the lives of countless others. It provides company when there is none, understanding where there is confusion, comfort where there is distress, and sheer, unpolluted energy where there is a hollow shell of brokenness and fatigue.

And so wherever and whenever there is the ubiquitous, knee-jerk temptation to roll eyes and tune out at hearing or reading the phrase 'classical music', I think of the huge mistakes I've made in the past by lazily adopting the principle of contempt prior to investigation. And to those of you who have that reaction, I urge you, beg you, to hold on for a minute and ask yourself this:

If there were something not manufactured by government, sweat shops, Apple or Big Pharma that could automatically, consistently, unfailingly add a little more excitement, lustre, depth and strength to your life, would you be curious?

Something with no side effects, requiring no commitment, no prior knowledge, no money, just some time and maybe a decent set of headphones.

Would you be interested?

We all have a soundtrack to our lives. Many of us have become immune, overexposed, tired and let down by it. We are assaulted by music in movies, TV shows, shopping malls, phone calls, elevators and advertisements. Quantity has long overtaken quality. More of everything is, apparently, good. And Christ, what a price we are paying for it. For every genuinely thrilling rock band, film score or contemporary composer, there are several thousand piles of shit that are thrust upon us at every opportunity. The industry behind it treats us with almost zero respect and even less trust. Success, rather than being earned, is bought, paid for, whored out and pushed onto us manipulatively and insidiously.

Among other things, I want this book to offer solutions to the watered-down, self-serving bastardisation of the classical music industry that we have been forced to embrace against our will. I hope that it will also show that the problems and potential solutions within the classical industry are applicable to a much, much wider panorama of similar issues within our whole culture in general and the arts in particular.

And woven throughout it is going to be my life story. Because it's a story that provides proof that music is the answer to the unanswerable. The basis for my conviction about that is that I would not exist, let alone exist productively, solidly – and, on occasion, happily – without music.

Many people would say that it is far, far too early for me to be writing a memoir. I'm thirty-eight (at time of writing), and the notion of an autobiography at this age might seem indulgent and egotistical. But to be able to write about what I believe in and has kept me alive, to expand on the ideas I've had for so many years, to respond to criticism and offer solutions to something that is troubling and urgent, is, I think, a worthwhile thing to do.

My qualifications for writing this come from having made it through certain experiences that some people perhaps wouldn't have. And having come out the other side (thus far) and, in the eyes of the editor who sold this idea to her boss 'made something of myself', I've now been given the opportunity to write a book. Which makes me fall about laughing because, as you'll see over the next 80,000 words, I'm surrounded by an inherent madness, have a rather warped concept of integrity, few worthwhile relationships, even fewer friends, and, all self-pity aside, I'm a bit of an asshole.

I hate myself, twitch too much, frequently say the wrong thing, scratch my ass at inappropriate times (and then sniff my fingers), can't look in the mirror without wanting to die. I'm a vain, self-obsessed, shallow, narcissistic, manipulative, degenerate, wheedling, whiny, needy, self-indulgent, vicious, cold, self-destructive douchebag.

I'll give you an example.

Today I woke up slightly before four in the morning.

Four a.m. is the worst possible time in any given twenty-four hours. In fact that hour between 3.30 and 4.30 is the absolute fucker. From 4.30 you're OK – you can kick around in bed until 5 and then get up safe in the knowledge that some people do in fact get up at 5 a.m. To get their idiotic jogs in before work, to get ready for the early shift, to meditate, to do yoga or have a blessed forty-five minutes not thinking about the kids or the mortgage.

Or just not thinking.

Whatever.

But if you're up any time before then, evidently there is something wrong with you.

There has to be.

I started writing this at 3.47 a.m.

There is something wrong with me.

I have seen enough 4 a.m.s roll by on my Rolex (fake), iPhone dock, IWC (real), grandfather, wall, auto-reverse/FM/CD player, Casio, Mickey Mouse (timepieces in reverse order) to last several lifetimes. There is the inevitable mental click, like a switch being flicked on, the 'fuck it' moment, when you decide to get up and on with it. To step up and step out into the world. Knowing it's going to hurt. That it's going to be a long one.

I know, for example, that I will have completed my four hours' piano practice, smoked fourteen cigarettes, drunk a pot of coffee, showered, read the paper, caught up on emails and filled the car up with petrol by 9 a.m. today. My entire day and everything that I needed to do in it will be achieved, over, ticked off by 9 a.m. What do I even do with that information? What the hell do I do from 9 a.m. until 11 p.m., which is the earliest I can turn my light off and try to go to sleep without feeling like a mentally ill loser?

And I know why I'm up so early so often.

It's all because of my head. The enemy. My eventual cause of death; land-mine, ticking bomb, Moriarty. My stupid fucking head that makes me weep and scream and yell and scratch my mental brain-eyes out in frustration. Ever-present, consistent only in its inconsistency, angry, spoiled, rotten, warped, wrong, sharp, honed, predatory.

Here's what happened this morning:

La Tête

A short play in one act by James Rhodes.

THE CHARACTERS:

A man; dishevelled, troubled, stubbly, skinny.
A woman; hot, blonde, too good for him.

*The man is lying in bed next to the woman. His eyes flip open next
to his girlfriend.*

She is asleep. He is awake and restless.

The clock says 3.30 a.m.

*With his extremely expressive face, he reveals that he shouldn't be
with someone as good as she is. Shouldn't be sharing a bed with
anyone. Shouldn't be this normal, dangerously intimate, quo-
fucking-tidian.*

The girl is too pretty, kind, generous.

The man hugs her. She doesn't move.

He reaches over and lifts her hair off of her eyes.

Man: I love you so much darling. I miss you. I want you.

Woman: *(croaky and still half asleep)* I love you too, precious
one. It's all OK, baby. Promise.

She falls back asleep

*The man starts to stroke her right breast and kisses her neck. He's
clumsy with it and desperate in a bad way.*

Woman: Mmmm. Can I have just a little bit longer to sleep,
darling? You're so sexy. It's dreadfully early still.

She falls back asleep.

The man stumbles out of bed passive aggressively, gets dressed noisily and shuts the bedroom door.

He walks into the kitchen and puts on the coffee machine.

Man: (*imitating her*) It's dreadfully early still . . . Fuck's sake.

Pinteresque pause

Man: (*walking about in a strop, to the audience*) She fucking hates me. Anyone else and she'd be fucking his brains out. For a really long time. She's probably taking care of herself right now, thinking about some asshole in the gym. Someone who isn't insecure and whiny. One of those dicks who is all self-assured and confident. Who can effortlessly get away with using the word 'fella'. Can talk about football convincingly. Find and use a stopcock.

He sits at his computer with his coffee cup.

Opens up a program, lights a cigarette, and starts typing.

Man: (*speaking as he types*) My love,

You're in bed masturbating over one of your exes or your boss or some other well-built, handsome cunt as I write this. I know you are. And so I have to punish you from the other room, using only my mind.

Sips coffee.

I know they're everything that I'm not. In my head I've imbued them all with a magical, effortless reality of 'massive cock and total genius'. I can't believe you're doing this to me. I am so furiously angry at you. So angry I am shaking. The adrenaline is flowing. My breathing is exploding. I am high from too much or too little oxygen, I don't know which one. I am right and you are wrong. I know what you are really thinking about and who and what you really want, and it cannot, will never, be me. Thank you for making it so clear to me. Now, once again, my world somehow fits. Order is restored and butterflies can flap away with impunity. Once again, anything that has threatened to make me less of a victim, a little bit happy, content, human, has been disregarded and dealt with. And it's not even ten past four. This is on you, you heartless, cruel bitch.

The man positions the computer screen just so. He pulls open the kitchen drawer, removes a knife and slits his throat.

End

That scene, that Brechtian fucking masterpiece — except for the last sentence because I'm too much of a fraud to follow through — was my morning head today. It plays out in a thousand similar ways each and every day and involves most people I come into contact with. It is how my head works, has worked, will probably work forever. Usually I manage to keep it to myself more successfully. Sometimes it comes out sideways. Always, it is there. And that is why I can't help but feel like I'm a mentally ill loser.

A quick caveat before you read any further: this book is likely to trigger you hugely if you've experienced sexual abuse, self-harm, psychiatric institutionalisation, getting high or suicidal ideation (the oddly charming medical term for past or present obsession with wanting to die by your own hand). I know this kind of warning is usually a cynical, salacious way of getting you to read on, and to be fair, there's a part of me that put it there for precisely that reason. But don't read this and then carve your arms up, spin out thinking about what happened to you when you were a kid, self-medicate, beat your wife/dog/your own face and then blame me. If you are one of those people then you've no doubt put responsibility for doing all of those things on the shoulders of other people your whole fucking life, so please stop it and don't foist your pathological self-hatred onto me. I have, from time to time, done the same thing myself and it is as misguided as it is pathetic.

The better part of me doesn't even want you to read this book. It wants anonymity, solitude, humility, space and privacy. But that better part is a tiny fraction of the whole, and the majority vote is for you to buy it, read it, react to it, talk about it, love me, forgive me, gain something special from it.

And, again, this book will talk, in places, about classical music. If you have concerns about that, then just do one thing before either throwing this book away or placing it back on the shelf. Buy, steal or stream these three albums: Beethoven Symphonies Nos 3 and 7 (you can buy all nine of his symphonies played by the London Symphony Orchestra on iTunes for £5.99); Bach Goldberg Variations (played on the piano by Glenn Gould and ideally the 1981 studio recording, on iTunes for under a fiver); Rachmaninov Piano Concertos Nos 2 and 3 (Andrei Gavrilov playing piano, £6.99). Worst case, you've paid for them, hate them all and are out of pocket the price of a takeout. Call me an asshole on Twitter and move on. Best case, you've opened a door to something that will baffle, delight, thrill and shock you for the rest of your life.

During my concerts I talk about the pieces I'm playing, why I've chosen them, what they mean to me, the context they were written in. And in that vein I'm going to offer a soundtrack to this book. In much the same way as fancy restaurants will suggest wines to accompany each course, there will be pieces of music to accompany each chapter. You can access them online at http://bit.do/instrumental – they're free, carefully chosen and important. I hope you like them.

Bach, 'Goldberg Variations', Aria
Glenn Gould, Piano

In 1741 some rich count (sic) was battling sickness and insomnia. As one did in those days, he employed a musician to live in his house and play the harpsichord to him while he was up at night wrestling with his demons. It was the Baroque equivalent of talk radio.

The musician's name was Goldberg and the count would take him to see J.S. Bach for lessons. At one of these, the count mentioned he'd like Goldberg to have some new pieces to play to him in the hope of cheering him up a little at three in the morning. Xanax was yet to be invented.

As a result, Bach composed one of the most enduring and powerful pieces of keyboard music ever to be written, which became known as the 'Goldberg Variations'; an aria followed by thirty variations and ending, full circle, with a repeat of the opening aria. The concept of theme and variations is similar to a book of short stories based on a single unifying subject – an opening story describing one specific theme with each following story in the collection somehow related to that theme.

As a pianist, they are the most frustrating, difficult, overwhelming, transcendent, treacherous, timeless pieces of music. As a listener they do things to me that only top-grade pharmaceuticals can achieve. They are a master-class in Wonder, and contain within them everything you could ever want to know.

In 1955, a young, brilliant, iconoclastic Canadian pianist called Glenn Gould became one of the first pianists to play and record them on a piano rather than a harpsichord. He chose to record them for his first album, to the horror of the record label executives who had wanted something more mainstream. It became one of the biggest-selling classical albums of all time, and to this day his recording remains the benchmark all other pianists aspire to reach. They all fall short.

I'M SITTING IN MY FLAT in Maida Vale. The dodgy part near the Harrow Road where kids are yelled at and alcohol and crack is Tropicana and cornflakes. I lost my lovely home in the posh part (Randolph Avenue, W9, natch) when my marriage ended – it was 2,000 square feet with a new Steinway grand piano, a big garden, four loos (shut up), two floors and the obligatory Smeg fridge.

To be fair, it also had bloodstains on the carpet, angry screams in the walls and the immovable, Febreze-resistant stench of ennui. My place now is small but perfectly formed, with only one john, no garden, a dodgy Japanese upright piano and the infinitely more pleasant smell of hope and possible redemption.

Among assorted directors, producers, crew, Channel 4 execs and whatnot, I'm here with my girlfriend Hattie, my mum Georgina, manager Denis and best friend Matthew. These four people have been here from the beginning, my mum literally, the others cosmically, or at least going back a few years.

These guys are the backbone. They're my Everything. With the notable and heartbreaking absence of my son, they are the guiding, shining forces in my life that represent the strongest possible motive for staying alive (staying alive) during dark times.

We're in my living room, pizza boxes strewn on the floor, about to watch my first TV show on Channel 4, *James Rhodes: Notes from the Inside*. It is a big moment for me. For anyone, I guess. But for me, someone who should not be here at all, it represents so much more than the 'look at me, I'm on TV' venereal disease that *I'm a Celebrity . . ., Big Brother* and Piers Morgan have infected us all with by continually fucking us in the ass via all media everywhere.

It is almost exactly six years since I was discharged from a secure mental institution.

I got out of my last mental hospital in 2007, off my face on meds, with no career, no manager, no albums, concerts, money or dignity. And now I am about to appear in front of an expected million-plus viewers in a prime-time Channel 4 documentary with my name in the title. So yes, even with the obligatory indignant, self-righteous, victim pout, it is a big deal.

All the more so because it could so easily have been a Channel 5 documentary entitled 'I ate my own penis to stop the aliens taking me. Again'. It could equally have been a CCTV excerpt from an episode of *Crimewatch*. But it isn't. It's something brilliant and honest and awkward and uncomfortable. Like a first date where you over-share (a lot) but don't care because she's hot and lovely and you want to crawl inside her and die from the moment you meet her.

The premise behind the film we made is that music heals. It offers a shot at redemption. It is one of the few things (non-chemical) that can burrow into our hearts and minds and do genuine good. And so I take a giant Steinway model D (the best there is, all £120,000 and 1300lbs of it) into a locked psychiatric ward, meet four schizophrenic patients and, after chatting to them, I play to them individually. They feel better, I look wistful, we all go on a journey of self-discovery and reach a better place.

So far, so TV exec wet dream, so vom.

But it is a powerful film. Pick of the day in every newspaper, and tear-inducing but not in a manipulative, ITV kind of way. The whole USP with the press is that I'm not just presenting and performing in it, but that it's especially poignant (their word) because I, too, was institutionalised and spent several months in secure psychiatric wards. They lap that victim-turned-success shit up. And, for my part, I love it. I'll do all the publicity I can get. Get in as many radio and TV interviews, double-page spreads and magazine shoots as I can.

As things build over time, I will use my backstory and minimal talent to flog albums, help charities, tour, do more TV and try to make a difference to those who don't have a voice. Those who are dealing with the darkest, most desperate symptoms and circumstances and have no one to hear them – the ignored, belittled, lonely, lost, isolated. The ones you see shuffling along in their own little worlds, heads down, eyes switched off, unheard and backed into a terrible, silent corner.

But I will also use it to try to make a difference to me personally. I will use it to make money and buy shit I don't need. Upgrade everything. Become visible and soaked through with attention. My head tells me I need this. That I hunger for it. Because at some level

I believe that there is a slim chance that (commercial) success, coupled with attention, will finally fix what is wrong with me.

And if it doesn't then I will go to Vegas, spend an aggressive amount of money in an even more aggressively short period of time and then blow my brains out.

We all watch the show. And I feel uncomfortable and exposed. Like listening to your voice on an answerphone for an hour in front of a room full of people. Naked. There's nothing quite like seeing your own name trending at the number one spot on Twitter while having literally thousands of comments, messages, tweets, Facebook updates all about you, to make you hunger for the isolation and security of a padded cell. It's the flip side of being an attention-seeking asshole – we shout 'look at me' for long enough and then when people do, we get confused and startled and moan about it. Shine a light on anything involving dodgy motives and it generally wants to crawl away in shame.

It goes down well in my messy little living room. Of course it does. We eat. They all say nice things because that's what you do if you're not socially retarded, and I get everyone except Hattie out the house, and go to bed.

All I'm thinking about is what a dick I look like on screen, all ill-fitting jeans, stupid hair, dodgy piano skills and ingratiating voice. How I should have prepared more for it and whether or not I'll get to feel important by being recognised on the Tube tomorrow. And then I get bored and angry at myself and force myself to think about the six concerts I have that are coming up in the next ten days. I do my usual night-time routine and, in my head, start going through each piece I'll be playing bar by bar. I check all the key ingredients that go into a concert – memory (in my head can I watch myself playing and see my hands hitting all the right notes?); structure (how does each section relate to the others, where are the important shifts and changes, how is the whole thing unified and related); dialogue (what's the story being told and how does that best get expressed); voicing (in a passage which contains several different melodies hidden among the notes, do I choose the obvious one or find inner voices that say something new); and on and on. It's like having a fucked record player living in my brain with an inbuilt music critic providing commentary; I start at the beginning of each piece and every time I make a mistake or my memory falters slightly I have to start again from the beginning. Which, with a seventy-five minute concert programme, can take a while. But it serves its purpose and stops me thinking about other things which, if I'm not careful, will take me down a road that leads to nothing but trouble.

I manage three hours' sleep. And the minute I wake up, it's on me. This thing that is more often than not my near-constant companion.

There is an addiction that is more destructive and dangerous than any drug, and it is rarely even acknowledged, let alone talked about. It is insidious, pervasive and at epidemic levels. It is the primary cause of the culture of entitlement, laziness and depression that surrounds us. It is an art form, an identity, a way of life and has a bottomless, infinite capacity for pain.

It is Victimhood.

Victimhood becomes, in a remarkably short period of time, a self-fulfilling prophecy. And having spent so long indulging it, it has its grip on me in ways that serve simply to anchor me further in the self-constructed hell that is The Victim.

When I was a child, there were things that happened to me, were done to me, that led to me operating my life from the position that I, and only I, am to blame for the things inside me that I despise. Clearly someone could only do those things to me if I were already inherently bad at a cellular level. And all the knowledge and understanding and kindness in the world will never, ever change the fact that this is my truth. Always has been. Always will be.

Ask anyone who's been raped. If they say differently they're lying.

Victims only get their happy endings in run-down massage parlours in Camden. We don't get to make it out the other side. We are ashamed, angry, appalled and to blame.

I sat there on that Wednesday evening in my pokey fucking living room, looked at myself on the TV screen being a massive, odious cunt, and realised that nothing has really changed. Deep down, like most of us, still now at the age of thirty-eight, I have this empty, black hole inside of me that nothing and no one seems capable of filling. I say like most of us because, well, look around you. Our society, our businesses, our social constructs, habits, pastimes, addictions and distractions are predicated on vast, endemic levels of emptiness and dissatisfaction. I call it self-hatred.

I hate who I was, am and have become and, as we are taught to, I constantly chastise myself for the things I do and say. And such are the global levels of intolerance, greed, entitlement and dysfunction it is evidently not just confined to a small, wounded section of society. We are all in a world of pain. If it was ever any different way back in the past, it has, by now, most certainly become normalised. And I am as angry about that as I am about my own past.

There is an anger that runs underneath everything, that fuels my life and feeds the animal inside me. And it is an anger that always, always prevents me, despite my best efforts, from becoming a better version of myself. My goddamn head seems to have a life of its own, quite beyond my control, incapable of reason, compassion or bargaining. It shouts at me from deep inside. As a kid the words didn't make sense. As an adult it's waiting at the end of my bed and starts talking an hour or two before I wake up so that when my eyes open it is in full-on rage mode, blaring this shit at me about how glad it is I'm finally awake, how fucked I am today, how there won't be enough time, I'll fuck everything up, my friends are plotting against me, trust no one, I must try as hard as I can to salvage everything in my life while knowing it's already a lost cause. I'm exhausted all the time. It's a kind of toxic ME – corrosive, pervasive, penetrative, negative, all the bad -ives.

I can feel it inside me now. I didn't realise how fucking angry I still was until I started writing this book. What a terrific smokescreen a bit of money, attention and media can be. How brilliant Beethoven is at distraction. Why do so many successful people keep going, moving forward, trying to outrun their demons by accumulating more stuff, more distractions, more noise until they fall flat on their faces and self-destruct? Because you cannot outrun the causes of anger as potent as this.

I can easily, happily look outwards to find reasons for my inner pain. I can make a convincing case as to why everyone in my life, every event, every situation and person and place and thing bears some responsibility for the fact that I am, most of the time, such a miserable, angry bastard.

And I can just as convincingly look inwards, turn the spotlight on myself, and have a party with the unremitting horror that is self-blame.

And it's all irrelevant, immaterial and pointless.

I all too frequently blame everyone and everything. I am at times so psychotically angry I can barely breathe. There is no way out and nothing that can ease it other than a few expensive, dangerous short-term fixes. And that anger is the reward for being a victim – every addiction needs a pay-off, and anger and blame are the rewards that sustain me and keep me going on a day-by-day basis.

Believe me, this overly indulgent mixture of self-hatred and whiny self-pity that I seem to be trapped in is not who I want to be.

I know that.

Who would want to be like this? Let alone admit to it.

I'd like to be all humble. Of service to music and the world and those less fortunate than myself. To bear witness to the fact that horrors can be endured and overcome. To help and give and grow and flourish. To feel light and free and balanced and to smile a lot.

But I've a greater chance of banging Rihanna.

Ultimately the reason I am so angry is because I know that there is nothing and nobody in this life that can help me overcome this completely. No relatives or wives or girlfriends or shrinks or iPads or pills or friends. Child rape is the Everest of trauma. How could it not be?

I was used, fucked, broken, toyed with and violated from the age of six. Over and over for years and years.

And here's how it happened.

Prokofiev, Piano Concerto No. 2, Finale
Evgeny Kissin, Piano

Sergei Prokofiev was one of the great musical revolutionaries. He wrote his first opera at nine, and by the time he was a teenager at the St Petersburg Conservatoire he was already established as one of the great enfants terrible of music, composing ferociously dissonant, virtuosic music that smashed down existing conventions around tonality and kicked music violently into a new direction.

I love him even more because he got reviews like this one from the New York Times: 'The House of Bondage of normal key relations is discarded. He is a psychologist of the uglier emotions. Hatred, contempt, rage – above all, rage – disgust, despair, mockery and defiance legitimately serve as models for moods.'

Awesome.

In 1912–13 Prokofiev wrote a piano concerto to the memory of a friend of his who had sent him a farewell letter and committed suicide. The music is so jarring, so angry, so overwhelmingly insane that when he gave the premiere many in the audience thought he was making fun of them. It remains one of

the most difficult pieces of music in the repertoire, with only a handful of
pianists being brave enough to perform it. One broke a finger while playing
it live.

It is the most accurate musical depiction of helter-skelter madness I have
ever heard.

I'M AT SCHOOL AND A bit fragile. It's 'big school' after all. I'm a
nervous kid. Shy and eager to please and be liked. I'm slight and
beautiful and look a bit like a girl. The school itself is posh, expensive,
on the same street as our house and, to my tiny eyes, huge. I am five
years old. I have few friends and don't really mind that. I'm 'sensitive'
but not retarded and awkward. Just slightly apart. I like dancing and
music and have a vivid imagination. I am free of much of the bullshit
that adults seem to be weighed down by, which is as it should be. My
little world is growing and unfurling in front of me and there is much
to explore at school. Again, as it should be.

One day (I was going to say 'one Tuesday' but it was over thirty
years ago and I haven't got a fucking clue what day of the week it
was) I went to the gym with the rest of the class. My first gym class
scares me. The other kids seem to know what to do. They can climb
ropes, hurl themselves at footballs and shriek with delight. I'm more
of a 'watching from the sidelines' kind of kid. But Mr Lee, our teacher,
doesn't seem to mind. He keeps giving me encouraging, kind looks.
Like he knows I'm a bit self-conscious but he's on my side and doesn't
mind at all. It's all unspoken, but it feels clean, defined, safe.

I find myself looking towards him more and more during the class.

And sure enough, every time I look up I catch his eye, and they sparkle a little bit. He smiles at me in a way none of the other boys would notice, and I know at some deep and untouchable level, it is a smile just for me. I feel like the noise and hustle and crowd recedes when he looks at me, and there's a rainbow-coloured spotlight shining on me and only he and I can see it.

It happens every time I go to his class. Just enough attention to feel slightly special, not enough to stand out. But enough to get me excited about gym class. Which is a pretty epic achievement. I keep trying to be nice for him so he'll give me a little bit more attention. I ask and answer questions, run harder, climb higher, never complain, make sure my gym kit is clean and smart. I know one day he'll come through. And sure enough, after a few weeks he asks me to stay behind and help him tidy up. And I feel like I've won some kind of lottery where self-esteem is the jackpot. A special 'you're the best, cutest, most adorable and brilliant child I've ever taught and all your patience has now paid off' prize. My chest feels swollen and alive with pride.

So we tidy up and talk. Like grown-ups talk. And I'm trying to be all nonchalant like this happens to me all the time and all of my friends are 130 years old and adult. And then he says to me, 'James, I've got you a present', and my heart stops for a second. He takes me into the walk-in gym cupboard where they store all the equipment and he has his desk and chair and he rummages around in his desk drawer. And then fuck me if he doesn't pull out a book of matches. In a bright red sleeve. Now I know I'm not allowed to touch matches. And yet here's this (achingly cool) man giving me some and telling me it's A-OK to light a few of them.

Kids are fucking stupid; it's why they're kids. He was overweight, balding, at least forty and far too hairy. But to me as a five-year-old he was ripped, strong, kind, handsome, dashing and totally magical. Go figure.

I ask him if he's sure it's OK and he again tells me to go ahead and light one up. So that's what I do. I light one and wait for the trouble, the shouting, the drama to start. And when nothing happens, when it's clear there is no trap, I go to town. Giggling, striking match after match, eyes wide and bright, smelling the sulphur, hearing the rip of the flame, feeling the heat on my little fingers.

Parenting tip – if you want a quiet half-hour to have a nap, give your toddler a book of matches. They'll be captivated.

It's the best thirty minutes of my short life. And I feel things that all little boys ache to feel – invincible, adult, 6 feet tall. Noticed.

And so it carried on. For weeks. Smiles, winks, encouragement, pen knives, lighters, stickers, chocolate bars, Action Men. A Zippo for my sixth birthday. Secret presents, special gestures, and an invitation to join the after-school boxing club.

Which is where everything went bad.

Now it's important to acknowledge that I chose to do boxing class. I was asked and I said yes. It was very much a conscious choice. It was not something that was foisted upon me. This guy, this movie star who I wanted to get closer to because he liked me and made me feel special, invited me to do something after school with him and I agreed to it.

You might think my five-year-old mind is a little unreliable. Not quite fully formed, not yet capable of accurate recall. So I'm going to let the head of the junior school speak for me. That way you'll know it's properly legit. It's from a police report she filed in 2010 and is unedited.

In September 1980, I was appointed Head Teacher of the Junior School at Arnold House, a Preparatory School for boys in St John's Wood. It was there that I first met James Rhodes. He was a beautiful little boy, dark haired and lithe, with a winning smile. He was bright, articulate and confident for a 5 year old. From the earliest of ages, it was clear that he had a talent for music. When he was 6, in about 1981–2, he was in my form (I was a teaching Head in those days). His parents were lovely people, themselves high achievers and they lived just down the road from the school. Although they recognised James' talents for music, I suspect they wanted him to have an all round experience in education and sporting activities were to be included. They signed James up for the extra curricular boxing activity. This was a paid activity and once 'signed up'; the parents committed to at least a full year of coaching.

Boxing was a popular activity with boys. It had been added to the curriculum by the previous owner of the school, George Smart. Many shiny silver cups were awarded for boxing at the annual Prize Giving. In the absence in those days, of a real Physical Education programme and having no Games field on site, as we were in the middle of St John's Wood, boxing in the early 80s was the only physical activity on offer and many parents opted for it for their sons.

The Boxing coach was a man named Peter Lee and I believe he worked at school on a part time basis in the late 70's. He hailed from the Margate area of Kent. He was a powerfully built man, but not very tall and was probably then in his late 40s. He seemed very 'old' to me! In 1981, the new Gymnasium was opened and Peter was in his element. He claimed to have been involved all his life with boys clubs and I clearly remember him boasting of his friendship with Jackie Pallo, who I gathered was a famous wrestler.

Quite a few of my boys from my Junior School were sent to Boxing to be taught by Peter Lee. Some appeared to really enjoy the activity and I do remember that in the beginning, James did too. However, fairly soon after he had joined the activity, I noticed a change in James' demeanour. He became rather withdrawn and appeared to be losing his sparkle. The boys who were down for the Boxing activity would change into the white shorts and coloured house T shirts in their class room and then I would escort them over to the Gym and then collect them 40 minutes later.

It became clear to me that James was becoming reluctant to attend this activity. He would take ages to change and often keep the rest of the group waiting. I remember so clearly the time he asked me to stay with him in the Gym. I didn't. I thought that he was being a bit of a wimp. However, every Boxing day, usually twice a week, James would play up and I realised that he really didn't want to be there. On many occasions, I did stay with him. I hated the whole thing. These very small children were positively encouraged to be aggressive. James was a thin little boy and it was clear that he was very uncomfortable. I thought at the time when Mr Lee asked James to stay behind to help him clear up the equipment that he was trying to make the child feel special. When I took the rest of the group back to change, it was always James who had to go with Mr Lee and help him clear up. I allowed this to happen on many occasions. This happened more than 25 years ago, long before Child Protection became an issue, but there seemed to be an element of trust between colleagues, and children being alone with an adult was never really questioned.

One day, James came back to the classroom to change having been with Peter Lee and he had a bloody face. When I asked him what had happened, he burst into tears and I went straight back to the Gym to question Mr Lee. I was told that James had fallen. I didn't believe him and at that point, I suspected that the man was being violent in some way to James. The next day, I shared my concerns with my colleague, who was the Headmaster looking after the Senior School. I told him about James' personality changes, that he seemed reluctant to go to the Boxing activity and that I was worried that Mr Lee was in some way frightening the child. He told me that I was over reacting and that little Rhodes needed toughening up.

I can't remember exactly how long James continued the activity, but I do remember him begging me not to send him to the Gym on more than one occasion. I also remember explaining, that because his parents had opted for this paid activity, I couldn't take him out of it without their permission. I spoke to James' Mum about this and she too had noticed that he wasn't particularly 'himself' and that he appeared withdrawn at home. She was a lovely lady who adored her 2 sons but I can't remember the activity being cancelled for him. I sat in that Gym week after week. I thought I was protecting him. One day he returned to the classroom after having helped Mr Lee tidy up and he had blood on his legs. I questioned him, but he never said a *word, just cried quietly. I took him home that day and we played the piano together.*

James left my care in the July to enter the Senior department. He no longer had me to protect him. It was frowned upon when the boys became 7+ for teachers to 'mother' them. I saw this once happy, confident child become paler and paler as time went on. He was a very unhappy boy and didn't stay the course until he was 13, but was moved to another school when he was about 9 or 10. My colleagues in the Senior School just said he was very unhappy – that was the reason for leaving.

I next saw James when he was 17 at Harrow School and competing in a Piano competition. My Godson was in the same competition. James struck me as a very troubled young man. I later heard he had had some sort of breakdown. I have recently read an article in the Sunday Times about James who is now an accomplished concert pianist. I was appalled to read that in the interview he referred to being seriously abused by a teacher at his primary school.

I felt sick with the remembrance of it. I am wracked with guilt for not realising the hell that James must have been going through. I tried to protect him from what I thought was physical nastiness. It never occurred to me in my naivety that anything of a sexual nature was occurring. I am in touch with James again. He has confirmed the sexual abuse and asked me to name the teacher who hurt him so badly. I got the name right.

Sadly, now I look back, James might not have been the only victim. There were several children who were fearful of Mr Lee and because of that I banned all children from my Junior School from going to his Boxing activity at the end of that year. I was regarded as an over protective female by my male colleagues. Thank God I was.

I am desperately sorry that James has suffered so deeply and for so long. I am also immensely proud that he has come through this and out the other side. He deserves every success and happiness in life. Scars and deep wounds sometimes make us stronger.

I write all this because I know I have to go to the Police. Mr Lee might still be alive. He might still be involved with children, even his own grandchildren. It is my view that he is a danger to young people. As a Minster in the Church of England and a part time Prison Chaplain, I see the effects that serious abuse has on the lives of young people. May God be the judge of these people who ruin the lives of others.

Chere Hunter

So there we are. My very own fight club. As Tyler Durden has taught us, the first rule of fight club is we never talk about fight club. And I didn't. For almost thirty years. And now I am. Because fuck you if you're one of the people who think I shouldn't.

There's quite a lot to unpack in the police statement above. There's a lot of insinuation but no real facts about the abuse. Abuse. What a word. Rape is better. Abuse is when you tell a traffic warden to fuck off. It isn't abuse when a forty-year-old man forces his cock inside a six-year-old boy's ass. That doesn't even come close to abuse. That is aggressive rape. It leads to multiple surgeries, scars (inside and out), tics, OCD, depression, suicidal ideation, vigorous self-harm, alcoholism, drug addiction, the most fucked-up of sexual hang-ups, gender confusion ('you look like a girl, are you sure you're not a little girl?'), sexuality confusion, paranoia, mistrust, compulsive lying, eating disorders, PTSD, DID (the shinier name for multiple personality disorder) and on and on and on.

I went, literally overnight, from a dancing, spinning, gigglingly alive kid who was enjoying the safety and adventure of a new school, to a walled-off, cement-shoed, lights-out automaton. It was immediate and shocking, like happily walking down a sunny path and suddenly having a trapdoor open up and dump you into a freezing cold lake.

You want to know how to rip all the child out of a child? Fuck him.

Fuck him repeatedly. Hit him. Hold him down and shove things inside him. Tell him things about himself that can only be true in the youngest of minds before logic and reason are fully formed and they will take hold of him and become an integral, unquestioned part of his being.

My mum, bless her, didn't notice or didn't want to notice anything was wrong. I don't blame her. She was a young, naive mother, overwhelmed with life and desperately trying to keep her shit together despite being a Valium-resistant insomniac with a family to look after and no rule book. It was all she could do to get up in the mornings, get food on the table and stay upright until 11 p.m. She was and is an incredibly empathic, generous and loving woman, and she was facing a horrific situation in the best and only way she knew how.

I'm not going to write about the sex in detail. For a number of reasons. Some of you might read it and use it to fantasise about. Some of you might read it and judge me for getting a boner at the time (on occasion). Some of you will read it and just feel nauseous and indignant. But most of all I don't want to go into detail because I don't think I'll make it out the other side if I do, especially when you can just buy a copy of the *Daily Mail* if you've the urge to feel titillated, nauseous or judgmental. Cheaper, quicker, less traumatic for me.

The point of sharing those sticky, toxic words is simply this: that first incident in that locked gym closet changed me irreversibly and permanently. From that moment on, the biggest, truest part of me was quantifiably, sickeningly different.

Schubert, Piano Trio No. 2 in E flat, Second Movement

Ashkenazy, Zukerman, Harrell Trio

A few months before his death in 1828 at the age of thirty-one, Schubert completed a fifty-minute-long trio for piano, violin and cello. He had led a short, miserable, broken life with music providing the sole counterpoint to his wretchedness. Schubert was constantly broke, relying on friends for food, lodging and cash. He was invariably unhappy in love, not helped by being short, ugly and over-sensitive to slights both real and imagined. And yet, despite being a walking, talking car crash, he was aggressively prolific – he wrote more than twenty thousand bars of music in his eighteenth year alone, composed nine symphonies (Beethoven had only written one by the age of thirty-one), over six hundred songs, twenty-one piano sonatas and endless chamber music.

The vast majority of his output wasn't performed until after his death, but this trio was. Chamber music was much easier to perform in private homes than orchestral music, and some homes in Vienna would host regular

Schubertiades – informal evenings of his music, together with poetry readings and dancing. In 1828 the trio was given a first performance at one of these evenings (put on to celebrate a friend's engagement). The slow movement encapsulates perfectly a life too short-lived – funereal and dark, tinged with hope and an insight into the infinite potential of genius.

Written by one of the only composers since Mozart who could conceive and compose an entire work in his head before scribbling it down on paper, this is the soundtrack of a man so depressed he started out his student days training to be a lawyer.

It is a devastating reminder of just how much we have missed out on by his dying prematurely at the age of thirty-one.

Stupid syphilis.

WHAT'S MORE INTERESTING (TO ME) than how I learned to swallow and take it in the ass, is the impact that rape has on a person. It is like a stain that is ever present. There are a thousand reminders of it each day. Every time I take a shit. Watch TV. See a child. Cry. Glimpse a newspaper. Hear the news. Watch a movie. Get touched. Have sex. Wank. Drink something unexpectedly hot or take too big a gulp. Cough or choke.

Hypervigilance is one of the weirder symptoms of PTSD. Every time I hear a loud noise, sneeze, bang, shriek, cry, car horn, anything sudden like a touch on the shoulder, a phone notification, I jump out of my skin. It's involuntary, uncontrollable, unintentionally humorous and dementing at once. And it's especially shit with classical music where sudden changes in volume occur all the time (if you see a slightly scruffy guy on the Tube with headphones on jumping out of his seat every few minutes, come and say hello).

There are also the tics. The little and not so little twitches that have been with me since the abuse started. Eyes twitch, vocal chords spasm, grunts and squeaks pop out uninvited and must be repeated until they are just right. And, continuing along the OCD/Tourette's spectrum, things need to be touched a certain way, rhythms tapped out impeccably on tables or walls or legs, light switches flicked the correct number of times, and on and on.

When I'm playing on stage is where it gets dangerous; if a part of my left hand touches the keys of the piano then I have to replicate the exact same touch with my right hand. I have to. And quickly, too. Which is not something I want to be thinking about and orchestrating when trying to remember the 30,000 notes of a Beethoven sonata. I will also need to sniff one of my hands at certain times while playing (a big ask). And I try (and fail) to pass all of it off as 'being artistic' so people don't notice. I will try and wait until I'm playing a loud bit before squeaking so the audience doesn't hear me. Will try, on the fly, to change the fingering I've spent hundreds of hours memorising to allow me to turn my hand inwards and scrape the edge of the keys to satisfy that unique itch. And God forbid I should see a hair on the key. Then I'll have to find time to brush it off, mid-performance, so everything is clean. It's a lot to think about, feels totally out of my control, and there is no satisfactory explanation that will cut it with the critics when it impacts on my playing.

The mental tics are much more insidious. Thoughts literally cannot be stopped or truly dreadful things will happen. So when I'm in a state, thinking about something bad, maybe about my girlfriend being all flirty with some other guy, or perhaps what it would feel like to hurt myself (a different variation on the same theme), it must be followed through until I am satisfied. So when well-meaning shrinks tell me to distract and stop the thought, I just laugh and think, 'Ain't going to happen, and actually you should thank me for it because if I do that you will end up paying the price and have some terrible accident, you'll lose your career and husband, end up broke and disabled and need your own shrink who you won't be able to afford so you'll die alone and in obscurity, miserable and afraid. You're welcome.'

Then there are the really shaming things. Like getting an erection every time I cry. Somehow the body remembers everything and links tears with sexual arousal. I would cry as he blew me. But physiology is physiology and my dick did its job and got hard. And so now when I cry it thinks, 'Oh I remember this! Up we go.'

Sex is an excellent topic also. The ground-swallowing, monumental shame of the orgasm. The images that fly across closed eyelids as you fuck, that force you to shake your head to try and make them disappear. The constant reminders of being touched there, there and there and what it meant at the time and so what it must mean now. The unremitting awfulness of believing at a core level that your girlfriend, wife, fiancée is somehow stained, broken, disgusting and evil because she had sex as a teenager. Despite knowing how ridiculous, how stupid, how illogical that sounds. I had sex young. It was bad. I am bad. You had sex young so you are bad. And so we cannot be together, I cannot respect you. You are so fucking disgusting. Marry me. I love you. You vile fucking whore. There's a Hallmark card, right there.

There were childhood sexual fantasies of being the sole survivor of a nuclear holocaust and wandering around the streets pulling women out of cars and doing unspeakable things to them, getting aroused at the thought of being held down and having to beg for my own life, and a host of other weird and wonderful kinks involving torture, control, pain and God knows what. All before the age of nine.

And those flashes of anger. Corroding, all-consuming anger at everything in the whole world. Anger at happy fucking families, broken families, families, sex, success, failure, sickness, children, pregnant women, police, doctors, lawyers, teachers, schools, hospitals, shrinks, door locks, gym mattresses, authority, drugs, abstinence, friends, enemies, smoking, not smoking, everything and everyone, ever.

Most of all, anger that I really, truly know that I cannot ever make what happened disappear completely. It's one of those hideous face-blot stain things that children stare at and adults look away from. It is just there all the time and nothing I do can or will ever erase it. And I can try as much as I like to make it 'my thing', the reason I am special, a permission slip to behave however I want and to feel like a wannabe, spastic Holden Caulfield even at thirty-eight, but I know all the time, every day, that there is nowhere I can put it, no way I can frame or reframe it, nothing I can do with it to make it bearable or acceptable.

There is an inbuilt mechanism in our psyche that helps with that, and it is dissociation. The most serious and long-lasting of all the symptoms of abuse. It's really quite brilliant. It started in the gym all those years ago.

He's inside me and it hurts. It's a huge shock on every level. And I know that it's not right. Can't be right. So I leave my body, floating out of it and up to the ceiling where I watch myself until it becomes too much even from there, and then I fly out of the room, straight through the closed doors and off to safety. It was an inexplicably brilliant feeling. What kid doesn't want to be able to fly? And it felt utterly real. I was, to all intents and purposes, quite literally flying. Weightless, detached, free. It happened every time and I didn't ever question it. I just felt grateful for the reprieve, the experience, the free high.

And ever since then, like a Pavlov puppy, the minute a feeling or situation even threatens to become overwhelming, I am no longer there. I exist physically and function on autopilot (I assume), but no one is consciously inside my mind. 'The lights are on but no one is home' is the perfect description. As a child that wasn't good because I couldn't control it at all, it happened all the time, and it meant I was labelled as spaced-out, difficult, gormless, not all there. I would wander around in shades of grey and disappear for ages. I'd be sent out to the shops to pick something up for my mum and not return for hours. When I did I'd be astonished at the panic and worry I had caused – time just seemed to disappear and I would have ended up hanging out with some random stranger or going somewhere entirely different from where I had meant to go.

Or today I will be chatting to my best friend and discussing, in detail, his plans for Christmas when five minutes later I'll say 'So what are your plans for Christmas?' Not that chatting with a pal about mundane shit is threatening in any real sense of the word, but it has become so in-built, such a part of me, that I often disappear, without even realising it, at even the barest hint of a threat. Like potentially having to commit to seeing someone at Christmas when it's only November and I may be dead, on holiday, busy, wanting to be alone and safe instead.

Key moments in my life are missing because of this. I look at my passport and know that I've been to certain places. I meet people who claim to know me, sometimes know me quite well. I go to restaurants where I'm welcomed back, tell people stories they gently remind me I've told them before or were there with me when it happened, and nothing . . . No fucking clue.

On the plus side it means I can watch the same movie and TV show several times without realising it; on the minus side I come across as rude, inconsiderate, a bit stupid. And it is fucking annoying not being able to remember almost everything to the point that it takes me several minutes to figure out what I had for breakfast, why I left the house, what day, month and year it is.

All the more weird that I can remember over 100,000 notes in a piano recital. All the more amazing that sat in front of a piano is one of the few places I am truly grounded.

I've been like this for as long as I can remember. As a kid disso-ciation was the only way the world could be vaguely manageable. If you don't remember you can't be terrorised by the past. Our psyches are fucking brilliant – designed to deal with any and all eventualities, at least until they are overloaded and break in two. And yet, even then there is often a way back to something approaching a working state.

And my closest friends are aware of it and they don't get upset when I ask them the same question twice in forty-five seconds or have no recollection of a holiday we took a few months or years ago. Which is exactly why they're my closest friends and why I can count them on the fingers of one hand.

Bach-Busoni, Chaconne
James Rhodes, Piano
(shut up, I'm proud of this one)

Bach wrote several groups of pieces in sixes – six partitas for keyboard, six for violin, six cello suites, six Brandenburg Concertos and many more. Musicians are weird like that.

There was a piece of music that Bach wrote around 1720 which was described by Yehudi Menuhin as 'the greatest structure for solo violin that exists'. I'd go much further than that. If Goethe was right and architecture is frozen music (what a quote!), this piece is a magical combination of the Taj Mahal, the Louvre and St Paul's Cathedral. It is the final and longest move-ment of his second (of six, of course) partita for violin. It is a set of variations (sixty-four of them, I counted) on a theme that drags us through every emotion known to man and a few bonus ones too. In this case, the subject is love with her attendant madness, majesty and mania.

Brahms said it best in a letter to Schumann's wife: 'On one stave, for a small instrument, the man writes a whole world of the deepest thoughts and most powerful feelings. If I imagined that I could have created, even conceived the piece, I am quite certain that the excess of excitement and earth-shattering experience would have driven me out of my mind.'

THE SEXUAL ABUSE WENT ON for nearly five years. By the time I left that school aged ten I'd been transformed into James 2.0. The automaton version. Able to act the part, fake feelings of empathy, and respond to questions with the appropriate answers (for the most part). But I felt nothing, had no concept of the expectancy of good (my favourite definition of 'joy'), had been factory reset to a bunch of fucked settings, and was a proper little mini-psychopath.

But something happened to me bang in the middle of all of it that I am convinced saved my life. It remains with me to this day and it will continue to do so as long as I'm alive.

There are only two things I know of which are guaranteed in my life – the love I have for my son, and the love I have for music. And – cue *X Factor* sob-story violins – music is what happened to me when I was seven.

Specifically classical music.

More specifically, Johann Sebastian Bach.

And if you want to be ultra detailed, his Chaconne for solo violin. In D minor.

BWV1004.

The piano version transcribed by Busoni. Ferruccio Dante Benvenuto Michelangelo Busoni.

I can keep going with this for a while yet. Dates, recording versions, length in minutes and seconds, CD covers etc etc. No wonder classical is so fucked. A single piece of music has dozens of extra little pieces of information attached to it, none of which is important to anyone other than me and the other four piano-mentalists reading this.

The point is this: in anyone's life, there are a small number of Princess Diana moments. Things that happen that are never forgotten and have a significant impact on one's life. For some it's the first time they have sex (aged eighteen for my first time with a woman, a hooker called Sandy, who was Australian and kind and let me watch porn while we did it in a basement flat near Baker Street for £40). For others it's when a parent dies, a new job starts, the birth of a child.

For me there have been four so far. In reverse chronological order, meeting Hattie, the birth of my son, the Bach-Busoni Chaconne, getting raped for the first time. Three of these were awesome. And by the law of averages, three out of four ain't bad.

I'll take it.

A few things about Bach that need clearing up.

If anyone does ever think about Bach (and why would they?), the chances are they will see in their heads an oldish guy, chubby, dour, bewigged, stern, Lutheran, dry, unromantic and in dire need of getting laid. His music is considered by some to be antiquated, irrelevant, boring, shallow and, like the beautiful architecture in Place des Vosges or Regent's Park, belonging to other people. He should be confined forever to cigar adverts, dentists' waiting rooms and octogenarian audiences at the Wigmore Hall.

Bach's story is remarkable.

By the age of four, his closest siblings have died. At nine his mother dies, at ten his father dies and he is orphaned. Shipped off to live with an elder brother who can't stand him, he is treated like shit and not allowed to focus on the music he loves. He is chronically abused at school to the point that he is absent for over half of his school days to avoid the ritual beatings and worse. He walks several hundred miles as a teenager so he can study at the best music school he knows of. He falls in love, marries, has twenty children. Eleven of those children die in infancy or childbirth. His wife dies. He is surrounded, engulfed by death.

At the same time that everyone he knows is dying, he is composing for the Church and the Court, teaching the organ, conducting the choir, composing for himself, teaching composition, playing the organ, taking Church services, teaching harpsichord, and generally going mental in the work arena. He writes over 3,000 pieces of music (many, many more have been lost), most of which are still, 300 years later, being performed, listened to, venerated all around the world. He does not have twelve-step groups, shrinks or anti-depressants. He does not piss and moan and watch daytime TV drinking Special Brew.

He gets on with it and lives as well and as creatively as he can. Not for the fanfare and reward, but, in his words, for the glory of God.

This is the man we are dealing with here. Drenched in grief, emerging from a childhood of disease, poverty, abuse and death, a hard-drinking, brawling, groupie-shagging, workaholic family man who still found time to be kind to his students, pay the bills and leave a legacy totally beyond the comprehension of most humans. Beethoven said that Bach was the immortal God of harmony. Even Nina Simone acknowledged that it was Bach who made her dedicate her life to music. Didn't help her so much with the heroin and alcohol addiction, but hey ho.

Clearly he was not going to be emotionally normal. He was obsessed with numbers and maths in a scarily OCD way. He used the alphabet as a basic code, where each letter corresponds to a number (A B C = 1 2 3 etc). BACH. B=2, A=1, C=3, H=8. Add them up and we get 14. Reverse that and we get 41. And 14 and 41 appear all the time in his works – number of bars, number of notes in a phrase, a hidden musical signature placed at key points in his works. It probably kept him safe in that weird way all those afflicted with light-flicking, counting and tapping tics feel safe. When it's done right.

Aged twelve he would sneak downstairs when everyone was asleep, steal a manuscript that his dickhead brother wouldn't let him look at, copy it out and hide it before carefully placing the original back where it belonged and going to bed for few hours' sleep before rising at 6 a.m. for school. He did this for six months until he had the entire musical score that he could study, pore over, inhabit.

He loved harmony so much that when he ran out of fingers he would put a stick in his mouth to push down additional notes on the keyboard so he could get his high.

You get the idea.

Back to the Chaconne. When his first wife, the great love of his life dies, he writes a piece of music in her memory. It is for solo violin, one of the six (of course) partitas he composed for that instrument. But it isn't really just a piece of music. It is a musical fucking cathedral built in her memory. It is the Eiffel Tower of love songs. And the crowning achievement in this partita is its last movement, the Chaconne.

Fifteen minutes of shattering intensity in the heartbreaking key of D minor.

Imagine everything you would ever want to say to someone you loved if you knew they were going to die, even the things that you couldn't put into words. Imagine distilling all of those words, feelings, emotions into the four strings of a violin and concentrating it into fifteen taut minutes. Imagine somehow finding a way to construct the entire universe of love and grief that we exist in, putting it in musical form, writing it down on paper and giving it to the world. That's what he did, a thousand times over, and every day that alone is enough to convince me that there is something bigger and better than my demons that exists in the world.

Enough hippie.

So in my childhood home I find a cassette tape. And on the tape is a live recording of this piece. Live recordings are, always, unequivocally better than studio ones. They have an electricity about them, a sense of danger and the thrill of a moment in time captured forever just for you, the listener. And of course the applause at the end gives me a little bit of wood because I dig things like that. Approval, reward, praise, ego.

I listen to the tape on my battered old Sony machine (with auto-reverse – you remember the almost magical joy of that?). And, in an instant, I'm gone again. This time not flying up to the ceiling and away from the physical pain of what's happening to me, rather I've gone further inside myself. It felt like being freezing cold and climbing into an ultra-warm and hypnotically comfortable duvet with one of those £3,000 NASA-designed mattresses underneath me. I had never, ever experienced anything like it before.

It's a dark piece; certainly the opening is grim. A kind of funereal chorale, filled with solemnity, grief and resigned hurt. Variation by variation it builds and recedes, expands and shrinks back in on itself like a musical black hole and equally baffling to the human mind. Some of the variations are in the major key, some in the minor. Some are bold and aggressive, some resigned and weary. They are by turns heroic, desperate, joyful, victorious, defeated. It makes time stand still, speed up, go backwards. I didn't know what the fuck was happening, but I literally could not move. It was like being on the receiving end of a Derren Brown trance-inducing finger-click while on Ketamine. It reached something in me. It reminds me now of that line in *Lolita* where she tells Humbert that he tore something inside her; I had something ripped apart inside me but this mended it. Effortlessly and instantly. And I knew, the same way I knew the instant I held him in my arms that I'd walk under a bus for my son, that this was what my life was going to consist of. Music and more music. It was to be a life devoted to music and the piano. Unquestioningly, happily, with the doubtful luxury of choice removed.

And I know how clichéd it is, but that piece became my safe place. Any time I felt anxious (any time I was awake) it was going round in my head. Its rhythms were being tapped out, its voices played again and again, altered, explored, experimented with. I dove inside it as if it were some kind of musical maze and wandered around happily lost. It set me up for life; without it I would have died years ago, I've no doubt. But with it, and with all the other music that it led me to discover, it acted like a force field that only the most toxic and brutal pain could penetrate.

Imagine what an aid that is.

By this time I had managed to find an exit strategy from the school of rape and applied to some provincial fuck-bucket of a school in the country. But I had now become a kind of classical music superhero – off I went to boarding school aged ten, piano music as my invisibility/ invincibility cloak.

It was a bit of out of the frying pan and into the industrial meat grinder, because I was by now a very odd kid, all tics and bed-wetting and spaced out and just weird. I threw up continuously on the way there, was so terrified I didn't speak to anyone for the first few days, was wandering round shell-shocked like some bomb survivor with his hearing broken and his brain still reverberating.

I was also the only Jew at this school. They literally had never even seen one before. I was like a science experiment – kids actually touching and prodding me to see if I 'felt different'. And they only knew I was Jewish because the cunt of a headmaster announced to the entire school at assembly one morning that I'd be absent for a day as I was celebrating the Jewish New Year. Which fell about a month into my first term.

But it didn't matter. Really it didn't. Because in comparison to what else was going on this was nothing. Regular beatings, blowing older boys (and staff) for Mars bars (I was more innocent back then – money meant nothing, sugar everything), torturing animals (newts, flies, nothing bigger that I can recall should that ease the disgust of the animal lovers amongst you), hiding, spending countless hours in locked toilet cubicles either bleeding and shitting or fucking and sucking. Throwing myself at older men and boys and doing anything they asked of me because, well, that was what you did. In the same way as shaking people's hands meant hello, offering yourself to some perverted bastard because you recognise 'that' look (paedophiles – don't think for a minute you're anonymous to those who've been through it) was absolutely normal and expected. Like being on holiday aged ten and going off with a dude in his forties (there with his family) into the toilets to blow him for an ice cream and still not classing it as abuse even today because I chose it. I gave him the nod. I led the way. I wanted an ice cream.

But I had music now. And so it didn't matter. Because I finally had definitive proof that all was well. That something existed in this horrific fucking world that was just for me, did not need to be shared or explained away, that was all mine. Nothing else was, except this.

The school had a couple of practice rooms with old, battered upright pianos in them. They were my salvation. Every spare moment I got I was in them, noodling away, trying to piece sounds together that meant something. I would get to breakfast as early as possible, before anyone else, because by this stage any kind of social interaction was too start-ling and fraught with danger, choke down Rice Krispies covered in white sugar, sit on my own and avoid any and all contact, then leg it for the piano.

I was shit, too. Not that it matters, but really, I was truly dreadful. Look at any one of a thousand Asian toddlers whacking out Beethoven on YouTube for the real thing, then imagine them with three stubby fingers and the brain of an Alzheimer's-addled stroke victim and you're approaching my level of skill. I laugh so hard now when parents push their kids up to me at CD signings post-concert and instruct me to tell them how long little Tom needs to practise for each day so that he can pass his grades and be proficient. My response is usually 'As long as he wants to. If he's not smiling and enjoying it then don't worry. If he's got the piano bug it doesn't matter – he'll find a way to make it.'

I found a way. I learned how to read music – it isn't hard and it's an essential first step. But of course I had no idea about things like fingering or how exactly to practise. Which finger to use on which note is, arguably, the most important part of how to learn a piece. Get it right and it makes your job so much easier. Get it wrong and it's an uphill battle that will never be fully secure in performance. There are so many factors to take into account. Here's an easy one, for example: what combination of fingers will make the melody sound clearest, smoothest, joined up and voiced as the composer intended, while still playing all the other notes and chords that are surrounding it? Some fingers are weaker or stronger than others and shouldn't be used in certain places; the thumb, for example, is heaviest and will make whichever note it hits sound louder than, say, the fourth finger, and so that has to be considered. The physical link between the fourth and fifth fingers is comparatively quite weak (especially in the left hand) and so when playing passages containing scales you should try and move from the third finger to the little finger, missing out the fourth entirely, in order to make them more even. Trilling (an ultra-rapid alternation of two notes, usually side by side, to create a vibrato, quivering sound) is easiest between the second and third fingers, but sometimes the same hand is playing a chord at the same time and so you need to trill between the fourth and fifth fingers to make every-thing flow naturally.

Sadly, the easiest combination to use physically doesn't always work musically (it can make things sound choppy or disconnected, uneven or unbalanced). Where a physical connection between two notes is impossible (too big a jump or simply not enough fingers) you need to learn to use weight to make the join sound totally connected, even if you're not actually physically connecting them. There must always be awareness not just of the note that you are playing but the relation of that note to what has come before and what is coming afterwards, and using the correct fingering is the surest way of doing that.

Sometimes you can play some of what the right hand is meant to be playing with the left hand to make it easier and vice versa, even if it's just one note of a chord – but it doesn't usually say that in the score and so you need to learn to spot opportunities to do it, mark it in the score, remember it, finger it, ensure the melodic line is still clear, that you're not using the pedals (which sustain and/or dampen the notes) too much, that you are in fact playing *all* the notes the composer wrote down, that the runs are even and balanced, the chords are correctly weighted (each individual finger must use a slightly different weight and force when playing a chord with five notes simultaneously), that the speed and volume are perfectly judged, graded and executed, the tone (how to use the weight of the hand, arms, fingers to make the chord you're playing sound a certain way) isn't too harsh or too soft, the wrists and arms aren't too tight, your breathing is right, the volume is measured and correct, and so on. It's like a giant maths puzzle where you get to use logic to solve it. But if you don't understand logic in the first place you're shooting in the dark.

The school I was at had a piano teacher of sorts, and he and I had a few sporadic lessons together, but he had no clue either. Of course he didn't – he was the music teacher who did everything and happened to play the piano at a pretty low level, and so he was the 'piano teacher' there. He knew as much about fingering, tone, breathing or posture as I did.

And all of this stuff is purely mechanics. The physical 'how to' of learning and playing a piece. It doesn't even touch on musical interpretation or how to memorise a piece. Christ, sometimes Bach didn't even specify what instrument a piece should be played on, let alone things like the speed and volume of it. Things got more detailed with Mozart and Beethoven as composers started to indicate those things, but even so they are merely signposts. There will never, can never, be two identical performances of the same piece of music, even when you're playing it twice yourself. There is an infinite choice of interpretation, and everyone has different opinions as to what is the 'right way', what is respectful/disrespectful of the composer, what is valid, what is exciting, what is dull, what is profound. It's entirely subjective.

And where to even begin with memorising approximately 100,000 individual notes so that even when phones go off, latecomers shuffle in, the wrong finger is accidentally used thus fucking up muscle memory completely, you are still totally secure. Some people visualise the score in their head, complete with coffee stains and pencil markings. Some rely on muscle memory. Some even use the score (which goes very much against the norm in solo recitals but is never a bad thing if it enables a great performance and removes crippling nerves). For me the best way is to play a piece through at a tenth of the normal speed without music because if you can get through it like that then there is nothing to worry about. Imagine an actor rehearsing a giant, hour-long monologue, going through it and pausing for three seconds between each word – if he can do that he knows it inside out and will nail it during performance. Playing it through in my mind, without moving my fingers, away from the piano and in a darkened room is a great memorising tool as well. Seeing the keyboard and my fingers on the right notes in my mind's eye proves invaluable.

And so learning the piano is maddening because it is at once an exact and an inexact science; there is a specific and valid way to master the mechanics underlying the physical performance of it (even this is dependent on physical attributes such as size, strength, finger span etc), and an inexact, ethereal, intangible route to find the meaning and interpretation of the piece being learned. And figuring out all of this as a vaguely retarded ten-year-old, pretty much entirely on his own and emotionally and physically fucked, was a bit of an ask.

I remember the first time I learned a full piece – the sense of achievement and total, utter delight I felt. It doesn't matter that it was Richard Clayderman's 'Ballade pour Adeline' (well to be fair it kind of does, I can only apologise) or that it was probably riddled with wrong notes. I had learned something, from memory, and could play it the whole way through. And all the arpeggios sounded fast and impressive and just like the guys on my tapes sounded, and holy shit this is the best thing that's ever happened to me. Christ how I wanted to play it to people, but there was no one there to get it, to hear it, to understand what it meant. I had to keep it just for me even if my heart was exploding with excitement, and that somehow made it even more special.

I was such a well-adjusted kid.

The only thing that came close to my worship of all things piano was smoking. Fucking smoking. The best invention since anything anywhere. This whole book could be a love letter to tobacco. The only thing greater than being on my own as a kid and playing the piano was wandering around hiding from the world smoking cigarettes. These magical cylinders with the most extraordinary medicinal qualities offered me everything I felt was missing. Getting hold of them was easier than you'd think, especially in 1985 – friendly newsagents, older kids, the odd kind (and horny) teacher. Silk Cut was my best friend.

I look at my life today and realise not much has really changed – Marlboro now, but cigarettes and the piano are the central things in my life. The only things that will not, cannot, let me down. Even the threat of cancer would simply be an excuse to finally watch *Breaking Bad* in its entirety and take a metric fuck-tonne of drugs.

The thing about smoking that they don't tell you is how good it is at stifling feelings. Later I found out that in several of the psych wards I was in, they actively encouraged patients to smoke as it made the nurses' job a lot easier. There is nothing as terrifying to a mentally ill person as a feeling. Good or bad doesn't matter. It still has the potential to turn our minds upside down and back to front without offering the vaguest clue how to deal with it reasonably or rationally. I am at least forty-three times more likely to top myself if I am not smoking. And so I smoke. Whenever I can, as much as I can. The odd occasion I've tried to stop has always been to please other people – the girl, family, society. Never works. I am a master at engineering a crisis that allows those close to me to grant smoking consent again. If there's a loaded gun (real or imagined) or a pack of cigarettes in front of you, take the smokes every time. I know that's off-message. But good God they work wonders for me. Even the thought of being able to smoke at a certain future event, be it a concert, party, interview, restaurant, keeps me on a somewhat even keel. Take that away (airports, for example) and I'm going to fuck your shit up. It's why I more often than not come back out through security for a last smoke and then all the way back through it again before flying off anywhere. Totally worth getting molested by the TSA assholes yet again. I'm not proud of it. I know it makes me seem like a wanker. A slave. A raging addict in total denial. I don't even care. I am all of those things and I will always be pathetically grateful for Big Tobacco.

So in a way, there were, on a good day, sufficient positive things to counteract the negative and I was happy enough at boarding school. I got into this cycle of terror (bullying, aggressive and unwanted sex, bewilderment) followed by the calm of space to smoke, play piano, listen to music. It reminds me of what it must be like for a soldier to come back from action to his home country for a few days before shipping off again. And this cycle continues unabated today. Terror of being on stage, of being intimate with Hattie, of seeing the psychiatrist, of being with my son and its attendant feelings, of being in social situations, circumstances I cannot control. And relief when home with a piano, locked door, ashtray, US TV shows, alone, uninterrupted. Time alone. The Holy Grail.

Beethoven, Piano Sonata No. 32, Op. 111, Second Movement
Garrick Ohlsson, Piano

In 1770, a child is born into difficult, violent, terrifying circumstances. His family is riddled with alcoholism, domestic violence, abuse and cruelty. Things get so out of control that at sixteen he takes his own father to court to wrest control of his income so that his family can eat.

While in his twenties, he singlehandedly drags music by the scruff of its neck from the Classical into the Romantic age, focusing on emotions, looking inwards, flouting convention, staying relentlessly true to his own convictions, composing for the orchestras of the future and resolutely indifferent to others' perceptions of him.

Totally deaf, wracked with pain, emotionally fucked, he composes his thirty-second and final piano sonata in 1822, a few years before his death.

It represents the absolute summit of his musical output for the piano.

Two movements long instead of the usual three or four, it manages, somehow, to transcend the level of human existence we inhabit and take us somewhere higher, where time stands still and we actually experience the concept of 'interiority' that he had spoken about and the inner worlds his music represents. This was music not for God or the Court; it was about feelings, about looking inwards, about humanity. ee cummings wrote that 'to be nobody-but-yourself – in a world which is doing its best, night and day, to make you everybody else – means to fight the hardest battle which any human being can fight; and never stop fighting'. Beethoven lived that every day of his goddamn life.

A WORD ABOUT TIME. BECAUSE it's important. Space is nothing without time. Time is a buffer. A safe space in between stuff happening. There is literally nothing as comforting to me as a completely empty day in my diary. No meetings, dinners, appointments, coffees with friends, dates, concerts. The knowledge that I can be at home all day with enough time to do whatever I need to do. It's the reason I arrive stupidly early to appointments, get to Heathrow five hours before my flight is due to leave, believe that a ten-minute car journey needs an hour. If there is enough time then I am safe. Needing six clear hours to do two hours of practice is about right. Same with every area of my life. Every album I've recorded I've been allotted three or four days' recording time and have used half of it. Exams completed within half the allocated time. Deadlines met magnificently early. Chores done in a third of the time needed. It's great for business, not so great for personal stuff. Dates don't want to order within thirty seconds of being given a menu and be done with dinner after forty-five minutes. They don't want to be next to someone constantly on the verge of a breakdown if they haven't left for a party round the corner two hours before the start, who is always the first person to show up, who they know when you say 'meet at 6' will be there waiting at 4.30, hopping from foot to foot like a slightly anxious meerkat.

I am driven by a hundred thousand different forms of terror. Terror of being criticised, of running out of time, of not being good enough, of getting things wrong, missing out on something, not being able to focus on other things that may come up, letting other people down. It is a constantly shifting, free-floating anxiety that no matter what is done to assuage it, will easily and quickly attach itself to something new I haven't even thought of yet. Like playing some David Lynch-inspired game of Whack-a-mole where every time you hit one on the head, a dozen more shoot up around you. And they smirk at you and say the most awful things and remind you of just how fucked you are.

I wake up with it. Always have.

If there were an ultra-neurotic Jewish mother, on coke, who was beyond evil and got wet off malevolence, that is that part of my mind. And so I hurl myself at the fucking piano as if my life depends on it. I throw myself into work. And from the outside I look like any other hard-working motherfucker who just wants to do the best job possible and not let people down. But the reality is that if I don't then I will die, I will murder, I will fall apart in the worst possible way. It is incredibly lucky that occasionally the urge for self-preservation looks like you have a decent work ethic. Fear, masquerading as humility and commitment to the job at hand, is enough to pull the wool over anyone's eyes.

And that's how I got through school. Terror-driven homework, panic-studying for exams, trying as hard as I could to make time expand and increase and cocoon things so that there was, at the very least, the illusion of safety there. I was a smart kid, too. The greatest benefit from being serially abused as a kid is the ability it gives you to read situations, minds, energy. Put me in front of an adult and I will know within a few seconds what they need to hear and see in order to feel comfortable and amenable to me. It worked brilliantly with teachers – depending on the kind of person they were, I was either homesick, vulnerable, tough, plucky, cute, flirtatious, needy or independent. And it got me whatever I wanted. Extra time in exams, higher grades, extra chocolate, leave of absence from PE, pocket money. Whatever. The point is that I figured out by the age of ten that I could be in any situation and survive, sometimes even flourish, because I have the manipulative power of a superhero.

Abuse sets you up for life to be a survivor. With that part of me that split off during the rapes running the show, I can exist with no money, no friends, nowhere to live and not only appear to be OK but actually appear to be thriving. During dark times friendships mean nothing; humans are seen only as routes to getting certain things – money, comfort, approval, a job, sex, and once their purpose is served it is on to the next one. The best 'friends' are the ones who I can keep coming back to for more and more over years – businesses always value repeat customers the highest, with good reason. Interactions are often simply transactions for victims of abuse. And sociopaths. That's why diagnoses are so fucking difficult – autism, Asperger's, PTSD, bipolar, various psychopathologies, narcissism, all share so many core attributes in the diagnostic manual. So I could be generous and say I have Asperger's and therefore I am quite manipulative and struggle with empathy, or I could say I'm a psychopath who is incapable of empathy. Both fit. Take your pick.

The problem, the great problem, is the following: while it serves a purpose, while you think you can remember all the lies, all the different characters you need to play depending on who you're with, eventually, after a few years you begin, inevitably, to lose track. It starts to catch up with you. And you start to doubt yourself. And that's when the trouble starts. You need to remember everything, and if you can't, or aren't quite sure if you're 'broken, broke victim' to a certain person as opposed to 'successful go-getter' then everything falls apart. So turning up in a brand new BMW for a weekend away with a friend who believes you're struggling to make ends meet requires serious explanation, more lies to keep track of, more information to retain. It is exhausting, terrifying and the stakes can be very high.

One of my diagnoses was dissociative identity disorder, where I have a number (thirteen if you're curious) of 'alters' who, depending on the situation, take turns to run the show. In effect that means I have thirteen people available as and when required, to do the job of one. It is like a military operation, and partially explains the memory problems, because the alters don't always communicate with one another effectively, if at all. Some are good, some are cold; all share one common goal – to survive no matter what.

There doesn't seem to be a cure, as such, for DID but it can be managed. The alters can be identified, acknowledged, talked to and made friends with. The less useful ones can be told to keep quiet, the more helpful ones encouraged to assimilate with the whole. That was a fun few days with the doctor.

And when it has got too much and I've had to walk away from a friend/relationship/colleague, when I've screwed things up because it all just got too complicated, it doesn't really matter because I can just start again with someone else, but it's frustrating to lose. Annoying to drop the ball and fail. Must try harder. It becomes almost a kind of game. And in a way it's sad because most of my friends and family genuinely love me. They believe they know the real me, and even if they've got doubts about some aspects of my behaviour or personality, they naively, if charmingly, believe that those doubts simply make them smart and empathic because they can see my many layers and still love me and understand me. But there is a complexity to things that people who weren't fucked as a kid just cannot understand.

Example – a girlfriend asks me a question. An easy one.

'What shall we eat for dinner?'

A Normal will answer, 'Chicken.'

Perhaps, 'Whatever you'd like, sweetheart, I'm easy.'

Or, if we're generous, 'Pick a restaurant, darling, and I'll take us there with pleasure.'

A survivor (especially one with PTSD or similar) needs to run through the following questions *silently* and in a split second before giving his answer:

Why is she asking?

What does she expect me to say?

How will she react if I do say that?

What does she want to eat?

Does she want me to suggest what I know she'll like?

Does she want me to suggest taking her out?

Why?

Have I done anything wrong?

Do I need to make up for anything?

What is the answer I want to give?

Why?

What will happen if I say that?

Is it a trick question?

Is it an anniversary?

What did we eat yesterday?

What are we eating tomorrow?

What do we have in the fridge?

Will she think I'm criticising her shopping skills?

What does she want me to answer?

What would her perfect guy answer?

What would a guy in the movies answer?

What would a normal person answer?

Who do I want/need to be when I answer this?

What would he answer?

Is that answer acceptable?

Is that answer in line with the 'me' she believes she knows?

Am I happy with this answer?

What is the probability she will be happy with this answer?

Is that an acceptable percentage?

If it fails, what is my get-out strategy?

Can I backtrack without causing too much damage?

What tone should I use?

Should it be phrased as a question?

A statement?

An order?

And on and on. In the blink of an eye. Kids at school who are being abused will take too much time to answer direct questions and appear evasive and startled. And they will be labelled 'difficult', 'stupid', 'ADHD', 'rebellious'. They're not. They're in some way being fucked. Look into it.

As you get older it becomes even more ingrained, like breathing. Sometimes, occasionally, it'll take us unawares. Especially first thing in the morning or when we're overtired. And so in case we're not quite bringing our A game when we're asked a question, we perfect the whole distraction routine: 'God you're looking beautiful', 'Fuck, my back just twinged', 'I love you so much', 'I was just thinking about when . . . (insert romantic memory here)', or more commonly, we stare into space pretending to be lost in thought and not hearing the question when in fact our brains are already racing to come up with a suitable answer. Anything to buy enough time to figure out the goddamn suitable answer.

We are multi-tasking, quick-thinking, hyper-aware, in-tune bastards. And it is a thankless, ceaseless, never-ending deluge of threat upon threat, fire after fire that has to be put out instantly. And because the body/brain cannot figure out the difference between real and imagined terror, they react as if we really are in the middle of a genuine war.

War is the best word to describe the daily life of a rape survivor. There are threats everywhere, you cannot relax ever, you take whatever you can get whenever you can get it because you are so scared of it not being there tomorrow – food, sex, attention, money, drugs. And you keep going on a mixture of adrenaline and terror. Morals go out of the window, the rulebook doesn't exist any more, you will survive at all costs no matter what. And living like that has certain knock-on effects. I cannot begin to tell you how fucked up the physical symptoms of abuse are. I spent years, decades even, almost chained to a toilet. As a kid at boarding school I was in there pretty much every night, usually around 3 a.m., in agony. Sweating and nauseous from the pain, feeling like there was a knife being twisted into my guts. Shitting what felt like water, too scared to leave the loo for at least two hours. Same again in the morning. I swear I got through childhood on around three to four hours' sleep a night. It's great for maintaining weight loss, not so good for socialising.

I know I'm going on about this quite a lot. But honestly, there's a lot to go on about. It is so easy to assume the abuse stops once the abuser is no longer in the picture and so hard to hear that that is only the beginning of it for those taking the abuse.

It didn't get better as an adult. That horrific feeling of being on a packed tube on the way to work, sweat pouring off my face, soaking through my shirt, guts absolutely wrenched in pain, not sure if I was going to make it to the loo in time. Sometimes yes, sometimes no. I could write a guide to the best easy-access toilets in London. I will, to the day I die, be grateful to luxury hotels. Shuffling into the Dorchester, the Lanesborough, the Ritz trying to look as if I belonged there and heading straight to the john just as my guts exploded in the warm safety of the locked marble-encrusted interior. Luxury hotels fit the bill only because they have multiple stalls and solid doors – Christ, Claridge's even has a white noise machine outside to preserve decorum. Popping into a Starbucks single cubicle for a terror-dump is a no-no purely because of the fear of a queue forming outside, noises being heard, judgment, stress, anxiety, not enough time.

I look at it on paper and feel baffled that I made it through boarding school, even with the help of music, fantasy and cigarettes. An anxious kid, shitting all the time, not sleeping, twitching dozens of times an hour, no social skills, terrified all the time, hooking himself out to strangers, smoking and drinking and yet this kid somehow made it to adulthood. It is a fucking miracle. And yet rather than feel proud, ready to seize all the bonus time I've been given, most of the time I just feel ashamed and pissed off that I'm still here.

Shame is the legacy of all abuse. It is the one thing guaranteed to keep us in the dark, and it is the one thing vital to understand if you want to get why abuse victims are so fucked up. The dictionary defines shame as 'A painful feeling of humiliation or distress caused by the consciousness of wrong or foolish behaviour'. And that definition breaks my heart a little. All abuse victims at some stage classify what was done to them as wrong/foolish behaviour that *they* have engaged in. Sometimes if they are incredibly lucky they can then realise and accept at a core level that they are wrong about that, but usually it is something that deep down they always, *I always*, believe to be true. The first family friend I told about the abuse had known me all my life. I was thirty when I told her and literally the first thing out of her mouth was 'Well, James, you were the *most* beautiful child.' More proof that I caused this. It was my flirtatiousness, beauty, neediness, sluttiness, evil, that made them do those things to me.

Shame is the reason we don't tell anyone about it. Threats work for a while, but not for years. Shame guarantees silence, and suicide is the ultimate silence. It does not matter how much you scream at them, *Good Will Hunting* style, 'it wasn't your fault'. You may as well say the sky is green. The only way to get through to them is to love them hard enough and consistently enough, even if from a distance, to begin to shake the foundations of their beliefs. And that is a task that most people simply cannot, do not, will never have the energy and patience to do. Imagine loving someone that unconditionally. Being that kind, gentle and loving so consistently and getting back rage, suspicion, paranoia, doubt, neediness and destruction most of the time. It is like rescuing a beaten dog from the pound who thanks you by mauling your kids and shitting on your floor day after day. It is a thankless task and one that, when it's even possible, 99 per cent of the time can only be achieved by someone who has had years of training, charges £200+ an hour in Harley Street and then goes home to his wife and kids thinking, 'Thank fuck I'm done with working with That for the day.'

I am many things. I am a musician, a man, a father, an asshole, a liar and a fraud. But yes, most of all I am ashamed. And perhaps there is a chance that I am those negative things as a result of being ashamed. That if I can accept, befriend, diffuse that feeling of blame, fault, badness, evil that is inside me, the defects and beliefs that seem to keep the world operating against me will fall away.

Scriabin, Piano Concerto, Last Movement
Vladimir Ashkenazy, Piano

Scriabin was a Russian pianist and composer. He started out writing lyrical, Chopinesque music and gradually became more adventurous, atonal and dissonant as he explored synaesthesia and the relationship between colours and music. He even invented an instrument with notes corresponding to colours called the clavier à lumière *to be used in his work* Prometheus: Poem of Fire.

He injured his right hand over-practising the piano, which somewhat forced him to move from pianist to composer, and from thereon in dedicated his life to musical symbolism and weirdness, seeing himself as some mystical, messianic character. ('I am God,' he wrote in his journal. A bit too often.)

He and Rachmaninov were the Blur v. Oasis of late nineteenth-century Russian music. And, sadly, no one was more famous during his lifetime, and few were more quickly ignored after his death than Scriabin.

His Piano Concerto, written before his shift to more far-flung harmonic landscapes, is still today criminally underplayed even though it equals, even surpasses, many of Rachmaninov's concertos.

I LEFT SCHOOL AT THIRTEEN and went to another boarding school. A hyper-expensive one filled with future leaders, captains of industry, despots, trust-fund crackheads and playboys. Harrow.

And I have to be careful here, because if you tell anyone that you were lucky enough to go to a school set in sixty acres with its own shooting range, theatre, cadet force and a staff-pupil ratio of about 12:1 and complain about it, they will feel, perhaps rightly, that you should shut the fuck up then and there. And the school and its facilities were excellent. Stupidly good. Offensively snobby and well-to-do. And yet I was exactly the same as I'd always been. Five years of the same shit – hiding in loos, same-sex promiscuity, locked in practice rooms with a piano, sick to my stomach, anxious and twitching.

I know. I'm bored of it all too. So much so that I'm going to skip this whole fucking five years and file it under the heading 'more of the same'. I cannot bear to write one more self-indulgent word about how much I struggled going to a £30,000 a year private school WITH ITS OWN SQUASH COURTS, CINEMA AND FARM in leafy suburbia. But there are two things I do need to talk about from that time and I'll try and keep them brief.

The first thing was I fell in love for the first time. And by 'fell in love', I mean I was catapulted into a maelstrom of feelings that I had never before experienced. It was the best kind of love, the only kind of 'first love' that exists. The love of mix-tapes, violent obsession, poetry and furious wanking all the time.

Cue yet another issue with being raped as a kid. It totally screws up your sex/relationship blueprint. For me that meant going on a first date with a girl and suggesting we fuck in the restaurant toilets in the same tone and with the same weight of feeling as if suggesting ordering coffee after dinner. It wasn't born of lust, it was simply what I thought to be the natural, normal thing to do. It didn't work (we were fifteen), but that look of horror on her face was one I got to become deeply familiar with. And it only served to increase the shame spiral and make sex seem even more squalid and secretive and evil.

But this first love wasn't a girl. It was a boy in the year below me who played the cello, who was beautiful and innocent and kind of like a version of me before everything went bad. Yep. I'm that narcissistic. And it was wonderful not because it was real (of course it wasn't), but because it provided a glorious distraction from my day-to-day reality. It liberated me from my own dramas and provided a focus for all of that pent-up neediness and emptiness that I was so desperate to fill.

My days were spent rushing around to the various places I thought he might be and, when I eventually found him, casually pretending I just happened to be there, sneaking off for cigarettes with him, and making immense efforts to memorise every last millimetre of his face, hands, arms to replay later on. When older boys and stinking men were doing me at night, his was the face I would be thinking of. It was a great obsession. One that lasted for the entire time I was at that school, and gave me a reason to exist. Which is exactly what a first love should do.

I'm not gay. Have never, since leaving school, had sexual contact with a man. But young love really is blind (and not just because it masturbated too much). It has no boundaries, no falling in line with what is correct. It just smacks you round the face and knocks you to the floor, delighting in your total inability to get back up.

Nothing ever happened between us and I don't even think he was aware of my feelings – another reason it lasted so long, I think – but it was a genuine oasis of good in the shitstorm that was my teenage years. It was a life raft of brain chemicals and fantasy, and constructing a potential world of him and me in my imagination was enough to keep me afloat.

Alongside the piano of course. By this time I'd got my first proper teacher, who was awesome, but crippled by having me as a student. His name was Colin Stone and he was, and continues to be, a total dude. He would let me smoke in his garden, indulge my ridiculous enthusiasm for all things piano, listen to me rant and rave until I was exhausted, allow me to attempt pieces I had no business attempting.

The problem was that I was sprinting marathons before I could even crawl. Trying to play pieces that were so far beyond my ability it was laughable, and yet somehow getting through them, carried only by a wave of irrepressible enthusiasm. The facilities there were second to none. Dozens of practice rooms, plenty of free time to lock myself away and play. They even allowed me to go out on my own into London proper to go to concerts. I don't think they'd ever had a student ask permission for that before and it became a rare moment of blissful freedom, trekking down to the Festival and Wigmore Halls on the Tube to listen to the great pianists pound the keyboard.

My life was governed by obsessions – The Boy, Bach, smoking. Every night I would listen to piano recordings of my heroes and stay up wide-eyed and in awe of what they were doing. I would plug in headphones and listen to Rachmaninov, floating away again with music and fantasy, imagining all the while that it was me playing. I found recordings by Grigory Sokolov, the greatest living pianist, that taught me more about music, life, commitment and passion than anything before or since has managed to do, and would listen slack-jawed and almost comatose at what he managed to do with a piano.

Literally the only thing in the universe I realised I wanted was to travel the world, alone, playing the piano in concert halls. The only thing. I would happily have died at twenty-five to have just a few years doing that. Everything else was a distraction. I knew I was irreparably broken, with no real chance of a proper career or family, but this felt, albeit through the funhouse mirror of denial and dumb enthusiasm, achievable. Musicians were meant to be all shades of fucked up, none more so than classical ones, who don't even have the luxury of ripped jeans, groupies and cocaine – they have to express their issues with stupid jumpers, non-existent social skills and deranged facial expressions, and I knew I fit the bill. All I needed was a piano and my hands and I was good to go. Social skills very much optional. It was the perfect career for me.

And the very saddest thing was that I knew at some level that I still wasn't good enough. I knew it. By the time they were my age, anyone considering a career as a concert pianist would have been playing pieces that I would never in a million years get close to playing. And they were playing them faultlessly. And although my lovely teacher tried his best (which included arranging for me to play to the head of keyboard at the Guildhall School who then offered me a scholarship), it was never going to happen. Not only did I lack the skills, my parents decreed it a no go. They would not support me should I go down that route, and insisted I go to a proper university. And me being the stupid, spineless wanker I was/am, I didn't tell them to go fuck themselves and go to music college regardless. I sucked it up and said OK.

How awful to have a passion so intense it dictates your every breath and yet to lack the moral backbone to pursue it.

The second thing I wanted to mention was that I discovered drink. I had been drunk before (the gym teacher and others used it on occasion to soften me up), but I had never actively chosen it, bought it, done it of my own volition. And that first time I did, aged thirteen, was the only thing that was on a par with listening to that piece of Bach. Half a bottle of vodka, falling down stairs, puking everywhere, ending up in hospital, being almost expelled from school, the shame and horror of my parents, the police interview (the vodka was stolen), all of it made not the slightest bit of difference. I had found another best friend for when the piano was unavailable. And I used it when-ever I could because it was like a magical elixir that made all the noise recede, made me feel 6 feet tall and indestructible, was the only thing that made my head quieten down a little, and was a guaranteed ticket out of my body and inner world within fifteen minutes.

Vodka and gin and occasionally scotch. I hated beer. There was nothing more comforting than finding a quiet place, hidden away, amid the madness of that school where everyone else was doing their fucking prep or hanging out with their friends, where you could sit in the cold night air with a bottle and a packet of smokes, feeling the wetness of the ground soaking through your trousers, seeing your breath escape in clouds that made trippy shapes. Whenever I managed to do that (perhaps once a week if I was lucky, increasing over time as I got older and had more freedom from supervision) felt like a three-week holiday somewhere warm. It was the perfect escape, and perhaps most importantly it helped me sleep. I would return to my room, everything spinning in the best possible way, fall onto my bed and fly away again. Just like when I was a kid. It meant that I was easy meat for anyone who wanted to use me (but then again I was easy anyway), but I was successfully anaesthetised every time I drank. And for that I will always, always, be grateful.

Alongside alcohol, I'd also been introduced to drugs around the age of fourteen. The damage that the gym teacher's cock had done had caused the lower part of my back to explode. Something so big being forced into something so small again and again cannot be sustained without causing catastrophic damage. I woke up at home one day in the holidays, vomiting from the pain, and was taken to hospital. Morphine and pethidine (heaven) were administered and I had the first of three back operations to repair the physical damage. This one was a laminectomy, as was the second one. The third was a fusion with titanium rods being put in my spine to literally keep me upright.

When I got to the hospital and was asked what had happened, I told them that I had been experiencing back pain for the last few weeks and it had got progressively worse. That no, it hadn't been caused by a fall or other physical trauma, but that I'd had a bad cough recently (smoking induced, though I kept that to myself) and that that morning I'd been coughing hard and felt something snap. I've no idea what my mum told them but imagine it was along similar lines. At no point did any of the doctors examine my ass or consider sexual abuse as a cause – they were baffled as to why this had happened in someone so young but put it down to a weak spine or a freak incident. Truth be told, I had no idea it was caused by the rapes; it wasn't until years later when I saw a proctologist (I'd been having severe pain in my groin and ass) that he told me both the groin problems and the problems I'd had in my spine were a direct result of aggressive sexual trauma as a child.

I just knew it hurt worse than anything I had ever experienced and I wanted the pain to stop. As the anaesthetist was asking me to count backwards from ten, I couldn't avoid thanking her directly for what was about to happen and looking at her with an expression of such gratitude that when I woke up there was a psych consult waiting who could not understand the raging boner I had for being anaesthetised and put under. Fucking idiot.

So it was the cigarettes, the alcohol, the piano and The Boy that powered me through my schooldays in much the same way as caffeine, a hot co-worker, porn and resentment get most adults through shitty jobs and disappointing families. They made the five years I was there pass by in a flash of hormones, altered consciousness and fugue states. And I made it. I made it through with good A level results (you cannot function at such consistently high levels of awareness, threat and pressure without higher than average intelligence and the ability to apply yourself consistently and vigorously), an offer of acceptance from Edinburgh University, and with the world, or most of it, still believing I was relatively normal, if a little weird and checked-out.

I left school at eighteen, feeling like sixty-eight, and realised that now I was an adult, the rest of my life could safely be spent destroying myself. People were no longer watching over me, I could spend as much time as I wanted to on my own. And the monster inside me was hell-bent on following through with that intention. My entire collection of personalities was raring to go, desperate to do anything and everything to fuck my shit up in as many ways as possible. And so I did. Hard.

It began in Edinburgh. To my mind a cold, windy, miserable city that seemed to be an exact replica of my inner landscape. I was high from the first day I arrived and did not come down until a year later when I was put into the first of several locked psychiatric wards and rammed full of anti-psychotics.

And holy shit, going on a drug-fuelled rampage was good. I mean, brain-breakingly good in the most sadistic, self-destructive way imaginable. I used myself as my own personal voodoo doll. Wandering around the roughest parts of Edinburgh and Glasgow at 2 a.m. looking to score, paranoia escalating dramatically, hearing voices, knowing that my room and car were bugged by the police, not eating for days, getting so high on cheap speed that I could literally not move for eighteen-hour stretches. There is a unique kind of powerlessness that comes from going missing for days, unnoticed, holed up in a grubby room, heart beating so fast you know it's about to explode, desperately wanting to call an ambulance but not being able to get to a phone in order to do so, resigning yourself to dying alone, mind helter-skelter-spinning, hallucinating things that have no business being imagined, pissing the bed, talking to yourself, shouting to yourself. You question your sanity and it responds out loud.

I very quickly stopped going to lectures, took so much acid that I could not distinguish reality from fantasy, smoked heroin (at once the greatest and stupidest thing I've ever done in my entire life), chain-smoked marijuana, bought vast quantities of speed and cocaine (ostensibly to deal, in practice to greedily shovel up my own nose), shoplifted, hid away and did not have a single friend. Not one. There was a girl who was pretty and kind. But after a week of being around me she rather bravely told me I needed a nurse not a girlfriend and that if I didn't stop getting high she'd never speak to me again. And she stuck to her word, bless her.

Most of what happened that whole year is missing from my memory. I have flashes: being followed by police; leaving to drive somewhere at 3 a.m. and being unable to figure out how I made it back home again; leaving London high as a kite in the middle of the night and managing to drive to Edinburgh in just over five hours (usually takes at least seven); trying, invariably unsuccessfully, to fuck a bunch of girls; driving the wrong way down one-way streets because 'it's quicker this way'; seeing a doctor who told me I had the lung capacity of a sixty-year-old (smoking class A drugs which crystallise on your lungs does that do you); wandering around the city in the middle of the night hallucinating and talking at strangers.

The side effects were unpleasant. Destructive, and because of that, rewarding, but unpleasant. And when I got home at the end of the first year and my mother saw that I had degenerated physically and mentally to beyond the point she could explain away to her friends as 'teenage shenanigans', I was sent to a psychiatrist. And I went without a fight. All the fight had been knocked out of me and it was just easier to do what I was told by this point. He spoke with me for about twenty minutes and made a call, and I was taken immediately to a hospital with locks on the doors and windows, silent, surly male nurses, and brilliant pharmaceuticals.

And so began my first psychiatric hospital experience.

How I wish psych wards had a loyalty card programme, with cards stamped for each day spent inside rather than each latte bought, where every tenth one resulted in a free day. It was a strange place, filled with stupidly young anorexic wives of millionaires, surly teenage children of rock stars and jaded celebrities fighting against the seductive allure of 'just one more line'. I was put on a combination of anti-psychotic medication, and after a few days began the excruciating process of group therapy, one-on-one counselling and whatever US-inspired method of treatment was currently in vogue.

After a week or so I decided simply to play along in the hope of getting out without being turned into an institutionalised zombie. I cried and talked about my inner child, participated in the twice-daily group meetings, shared my feelings of inadequacy and my faux-heartfelt desire to change and stop getting high.

And sure enough it worked. I was making 'tremendous progress' and was released back into society after five weeks, my little booklet of NA/AA meetings under my arm.

Edinburgh had made it very clear I would not be welcome back there – apparently turning up to exams visibly high and being offensive to lecturers was a bridge too far, and so I packed my bags and went to Paris. A year of French girls, learning a new language and that brilliant, über-middle-class word, 'rest', seemed like an excellent idea.

To recap, poor Jimmy goes from a £30k-a-year private school to university, where he doesn't have a good time. He ends up in a psychiatric hospital paid for by his medical insurance, gets out and goes to Paris to recover by hanging out for a year in one of the most beautiful cities in the world and learning French.

You're no doubt weeping for him already.

I got a job at Burger King grilling les Whoppers, rented a flat that was so small there was a cooker in the bathroom and when the bed folded out I could literally climb across the entire room from front door to far wall without getting off it, and decided to stop drinking and using drugs.

And I've got to say it was, perhaps unsurprisingly, one of the best twelve months of my life. There was a succession of girls (the best way to learn French), hundreds of French Narcotics Anonymous meetings (the second-best way to learn French), middle-of-the-night chess games, nights spent dancing in loud, sweaty clubs, new friends and a slow accumulation of days without alcohol or drugs of any kind. Could anyone be miserable in Paris? I've yet to see a fat Parisienne, the city has the heart-stoppingly beautiful architecture that can only come from surrendering to enemy forces in the early days of war, art, coffee, crêpes, husky accents, a natural disdain for work, and smoking everywhere.

I had some tricky moments staying clean – a couple of sly drinks thinking that perhaps I could do it in moderation, and quickly realising that getting pissed at 3 a.m. and wandering around the dodgier parts of Paris trying to score heroin wasn't necessarily healthy. About halfway through my time in Paris, somehow, miraculously, I poured away the rest of my last ever drink on 29 March 1995 and, through the gentle miracle that is twelve-step groups, stayed clean and sober.

And overall things improved dramatically.

The voices stopped (auditory hallucinations are a common side effect of both psychotropic drugs and trauma), the madness receded and I had a glimpse of a life that seemed fun, frivolous, even manageable. I bought a little electronic keyboard (the idea of a real piano fitting in that flat was preposterous) and did the best I could with it, but I was starting to realise that any dream of making a career out of playing the piano was simply too far-fetched. I might as well have wanted to become an astronaut. And so I just stopped playing completely. I distracted myself with anything I could that wasn't chemical, and was determined to make up for all the lost years of isolation and terror by resolutely trying to cram a whole reclaimed teenage life into a year. And then I applied to a bunch of universities in London with the aim of reading psychology.

Shut up, it's true.

What was rather lovely is that I wrote to seven universities saying that I'd just got out of a psych ward where I had been successfully treated for drug-induced psychosis and was keen to study psychology at their fine institution etc etc, that I knew I had missed the application deadline and that Edinburgh would not be providing any references but please could I come because I'm all better now? And five of them said yes without any further prompting, let alone interviews. My gift for bullshit manipulation was still golden.

And after a year of, literally, fucking around, I came back to London, fluent in French, and waltzed through the doors of University College London. Still clean and sober. Still nuts (in remission, perhaps, but nuts). Still running from a childhood which by now I had semi-successfully buried pretty deep down.

Here's another side note for anyone who went through similar childhood trauma: you cannot outrun this stuff.

You cannot hide from it.

You cannot deny it.

You cannot push it down and expect it not to eventually reappear.

Had I known what was going to happen to me down the line I would have happily checked into any psych ward in the world for a year to deal with it, no matter what it cost in money and time and lost opportunities. The grief I would have saved myself from by taking a few months out to work on my stuff (a kind of gap year for mental people) would have been immeasurable. But I was stupidly, blissfully, idiotically oblivious. I figured if I could manage not to think about things, deny everything bad, distract and avoid, I would be immune to the past. It would, like a body buried under the patio, in time decay and disappear, albeit with a bit of a lingering smell. And so I focused on being a good student, tried my utmost to avoid self-examination, and got on with day-to-day life.

It was a dull, albeit semi-productive, three years. I had swapped the piano, alcohol and drugs for girlfriends and hookers and completed my assignments, hidden myself away in the arms of another blonde, brunette, whatever, and got to the end of the course. I adopted the persona of a grandiose, slightly freaky douchebag to keep people at arm's length, and was utterly uninterested in any kind of social life or self-improvement.

I did however manage to begin and maintain a relationship with Matthew, the man who became my closest friend. I knew instantly that he was safe. He was tall, stupidly handsome, brilliant and kind.

And those qualities have only grown over time. The guy is a psychologist who holds two PhDs and does vital, life-changing work. And he just doesn't care that I forget things (birthdays, plans, social niceties like asking about his news etc), sometimes come across as rude and insensitive, get needy and weird and can suddenly go quiet on him for no reason.

He was my first friend.

He is still my best friend and worth a thousand vague acquaintances I could have made at university.

I walked away with a semi-respectable 2:1, didn't go to graduation, and then, because it was time to earn some money, I opened the *Evening Standard*, applied for the first sales vacancy I saw (financial publishing) and, after a brief ten-minute interview, got the job.

Ravel, Piano Trio

Vladimir Ashkenazy, Itzhak Perlman, Lynn Harrell

Ravel was an asexual, mother-obsessed Frenchman who wrote fewer than ninety compositions during the course of his life. The son of a Swiss inventor and a Basque mother, he was a chain-smoking dandy who sweated blood over his music and had each note dragged out of him painfully, slowly and methodically. He and Debussy were the greatest exponents of Impressionist music France ever produced and despite being somewhat fucked by the trauma of serving as a truck driver during the First World War and later suffering brain damage from a collision with a Parisian taxi, he remains the towering genius of French music.

Hanging out with Gershwin in Harlem jazz clubs lent a certain swagger to his music.

His piano trio is a force of nature; visceral, energetic and somehow much bigger than the three instruments it was written for, it was the last piece he wrote before enlisting in the army. Four movements long and demanding an almost superhuman level of virtuosity from the performers, it's a swirling, whirling kaleidoscope of colours and dreams. He said that the only love affair he had ever had was with music, and all of that repressed sexual energy got thrown into the mix as a result.

IF THIS WERE A MOVIE, I'd freeze-frame it right about now. This was a huge turning point for me, even if I had no clue what was really happening in my life. Ostensibly it all seemed normal. Complete your studies, get a degree, get a job, start out on a career path, fall in love, get married, start a family. This was what was happening to me and I was unaware, incapable of stopping it. I was labouring under the totally misguided belief that someone like me, with my history and my head, could pull this off. Breaking myself, wallowing in victimhood, fucking shit up – yes, absolutely. Being a stand-up, productive, normalised member of society? Not so much. In the movie I'd make it go all *Sliding Doors* style and go down another route totally opposite to the stupid bloody route I'd chosen. And I'd see very quickly that doing pretty much anything other than pretending to be normal would have been a safer bet.

But I didn't. All my own fault. Even if some guy from the future had stood in front of me shrieking at me to do something different and doing a Ghost of Christmas Yet to Come on me I wouldn't have believed him. Because I'd long ago, consciously or otherwise, started running away from myself and what was real for me, and by now I couldn't change course even if I'd wanted to. There is a horrible irony in knowing that I spent most of my life running away from the things that would ultimately save me (honesty, truth, reality, love, self-acceptance) because I believed they would kill me.

So there I was, propelling myself forward and using terror as fuel. Still no piano, no self-examination, no past, no concept of who I am or what I was. I was on autopilot. And, fuck me, it is still amazing to me how easy it was to pull off.

My job involved selling advertising and editorial to businesses around the world for financial publications no one read. And as it involved manipulating, lying to and cajoling older men, I was absolutely amazing at it. I was earning commission on every sale, alongside a small basic salary, and while my friends were starting off on £20,000 a year, I was pulling in £3,000 to £4,000 per week without breaking a sweat, working until 5 p.m. every day and never on weekends. Admittedly, my weird time neurosis meant I was in the office by 7.30 a.m. every day, my desperate need to succeed and appear to be number one helped drive me, and the money made me hungry for more.

If there is a career designed both to feed self-hatred of unimaginable proportions, while also stroking fragile egos, working in the City fits the bill better than most others. Especially as I was clean and sober – all that money for a single guy aged twenty-two was guaranteed to buy me a few years of distraction and evasion. I took girls to the most expensive hotels, bought them unimaginably stupid presents, travelled around the world, had suits made for me, ate in restaurants where the first course alone cost more than a meal for four at Pizza Express. I was a massive, catastrophic cock. A parody of everything bad about the rat race and the human race.

And here's another cool thing about abuse – the body never forgets. So I could run as fast as I liked, distract myself as much as possible, but every fucking day I was practically shitting myself with anxiety on the Tube, my body was falling apart, my muscles were like taut, creaking old ropes, my head felt like it was in a vice for sixteen hours a day. And once again my back fell apart.

I had operation number two, enjoyed the dubious thrill of A-grade narcotics after a few years of being clean, and rushed straight back into my life of denial.

And then I met the woman who was to become my wife. The poor thing didn't stand a chance. I didn't have girlfriends, I took hostages. And Jane (at her request I have agreed to use a pseudonym) was the perfect candidate. She was pretty, ten years older than me, had been married twice before and seemed to have escaped from the 1920s world of Gatsby, prohibition and big parties. I was, in all truth, looking for a mother; she was, well, I've no idea what she was looking for, but it could not have been me unless this was some massively inappropriate cosmic joke.

I think she simply wanted a husband who wasn't an asshole. And I, cruelly if subconsciously, played right into that. I hurled Tiffany at her, took her away for weekends at the George V in Paris, sent her flowers three times a week, insisted she move from her shitty bedsit in Streatham to my flat after just two months, paid for everything and did everything I could to play the role of 'awesome suitor'. And I did it despite myself. Despite knowing it was likely a huge mistake. Despite knowing that this was not me, that I was incapable of a relationship. I wanted to rescue her, feel good about myself for doing so, and live this Disneyfied fucking fairytale existence. And it was a disaster. I knew it was going to implode, that it was unsustainable. And so I asked her to marry me. Because that was what you did after eleven months with someone, that is what normal people did, that would balance out the crazy in me, that would add a layer of ordinary to my life.

We got engaged. My body kept sending me messages to stop. I had yet another back operation, a big, fuck-off, serious spinal fusion.

We got married. I cried during my speech because I couldn't find a way to stop things inexorably moving forward. Two days later, 9/11 happened. Our honeymoon was overpriced and hollow. I got stung by a wasp on my ass. I woke up in our bridal suite in some exotic hotel in the South of France, realised I was now married, and somewhere far away, something horrible started to laugh and laugh and laugh.

I've honestly no idea what I was thinking, beyond that rather sad hope that if I continued to do what normal people did then I would somehow become normal. But the idea that a man like me could not only get married, but maintain, nurture, commit to a marriage was fucking ridiculous. My whole concept of love was skewed. Love for me was attention, sympathy, point-scoring, based on external opinions and external, material things. It was not about shared values and shared beliefs. It was naive, dysfunctional, unhealthy and selfish. It was a child's love for a parent, not a man's for his wife. And it is a challenge to write about this stuff without wanting to punch myself in the face again and again until there's nothing left. But it is what it is.

We made a 'perfect home' with ridiculously expensive furniture. It looked beautiful and felt vacuum-packed. I threw money around and did all I could to distract us from the inherent flaw with our marriage which was that I (I cannot, will not speak for her) was totally, utterly incapable of maintaining a functional relationship. She was, is, a really lovely woman. She is kind and compassionate, empathic and funny, and she has a brilliant mind.

And then she fell pregnant. It was a long and clumsy and painful fall. Something cataclysmic seemed to have happened even though nothing tangible had changed and I started falling deeper and deeper into despair and panic at what was about to happen. My world was on an unstoppable collision course with forces unseen and magnificent in their strength as I scrabbled about pretending to be one person, knowing I was quite another. And here's probably a good time to pause for yet another moment.

Shostakovich, Piano Concerto No. 2, Second Movement

Elisabeth Leonskaja, Piano

In 1957 the titan of Russian music, Dmitri Shostakovich, wrote his second piano concerto for his son's birthday. Perhaps because of who it was written for, it proved something of a break from his usual sardonic, angry, oppressive style (listen to his fifth and greatest symphony for a definitive example of this).

Unlike almost all of his contemporaries, Shostakovich remained in Russia for his entire life, despite the turmoil and Stalinist madness that caused Prokofiev, Rachmaninov et al to leave. He stayed and fought through music, occasionally using his compositions to portray musical parodies of a fucked State.

He was driven, political, fearless and revolutionary, saying, rather beautifully, 'A creative artist works on his next composition because he was not satisfied with his previous one.'

This slow movement, with echoes of Beethoven's 'Emperor' Concerto, remains one of his most romantic and beautiful compositions, all the more so given the horrors that were occurring all around him while he was writing it.

ANNOUNCING PREGNANCY IS AN ALMOST universal cause for celebration. Fatherhood has become a kind of sanitised paean to the miraculous. It comprises mental stock images of smiling fathers hoisting gurgling babies onto their shoulders and walking arm and arm with their wives through parks. We make light of the lack of sleep, the excruciating responsibility of creating life, the expense, mess, emotional strain of having children. Books are written with titles like 'I fall asleep at red lights – the story of the man who had triplets'. There are countless guides to 'effective parenting' whatever the fuck that means. The reality, for me at least, was something far more sinister.

My son was and is a miracle. There is nothing I will experience in my life that will ever match the incandescent atomic bomb of love that exploded in me when he was born. I did not understand the word 'perfection' until I held him in my arms. Nor did I fully appreciate the concept of God. And if any fathers are reading this who claim not to believe in God then you are lying. Because I promise you, when you're waiting in the hospital, wife in labour, doctors and nurses bustling around, the smell of ammonia seeping into your nostrils, there is only one thought going through your mind – 'please God let him be healthy. I don't care if he's not that smart, athletic, handsome, talented. Just give him ten fingers and ten toes'.

But for me there was a flip side to this. There had to be. Something that powerful has to have an equally intense opposite to counterbalance it. And for me it was terror. Pure, unadulterated, visceral terror. I had been handed the most precious thing in the world and in my core, I knew that I was fundamentally incapable of meeting that responsibility.

You can leave a marriage, quit a job, sell a home, justifiably walk away from your friends, family, exes, rehome a pet. But a child? A biological extension of your very soul? There is simply no escape from that.

Jack (a pseudonym, again at Jane's request) was the most extraordinary child. Every parent says that about their kids. And to you he was probably just another shitting, crying, moaning, kind of cute little thing. But to me he was, is, always will be shattering proof of all that is magical in this world. Despite my feelings about our marriage, he was conceived from a place of love and desire. He was wanted, desperately wanted, and from the get-go he was adored and admired and awesome and astounding and all the As there are.

And yet. There were so many messy things that had happened to me in my life that I had been too short-sighted, lazy or scared (take your pick) to clean up before he came along. And because of that he had an introduction to this world that was harder than most. A four-year-old having a father who spent nine months in psychiatric hospitals does not have a father in any real sense of the word. An infant having a father who had not even remotely conquered his particular brand of crazy does not have a father. Deciding to create life before being absolutely certain that I had the skills necessary to do that responsibly is an almost unforgivable transgression and yet that is exactly what I did.

I had a list of qualities I wanted to embody as a father. It included words like strong, available, ever-present, patient, secure, married, loving. And I fell far short on all of them save for that last one. Loving. And such was the power of biology, the universe, genes, the heart, nature, loving my son was and is the easiest, most natural thing in the world to me. I struggle to do it for myself, my friends, girlfriends, even family. But with Jack? It is like breathing.

As I've started to battle some of my past demons, there are things that I'm able to offer him now, albeit a little behind schedule. He'll never have to worry about doing a job that 'looks right'. He will only ever need to consider doing something that makes him laugh, jump up and down with excitement and want to tell the whole world about. And if he can't earn enough money from that to live comfortably I will happily pick up the slack and support him for as long as is necessary. The only thing that I want for him, much more than academic or financial success, is to be relentless in his pursuit of laughter and joy.

I want him to know the secret of happiness. It is so simple that it seems to have eluded many people. The trick is to do whatever you want to do that makes you happy, as long as you're not hurting those around you. Not to do what you think you should be doing. Nor what you think other people believe you should be doing. But simply to act in a way that brings you immense joy. To be able to say a gentle and kind 'no' to things that don't please you, to walk away from situations that don't fulfil you, to move towards things that delight you. And there is nothing I will not do in order to help him achieve that.

I don't think I will ever be able to make my peace with the fact that the ripples of my past became tidal waves when he was born. It doesn't matter at all that I didn't have the luxury of choice when it came to losing my shit and breaking down. That I would have walked through fire for eternity to spare him having a father who was absent, fucked, a disgrace, a shadow of what a father should be. Saying sorry to him is as empty and as hollow a gesture as I can think of. The one slim shot I have of making it sincere in his eyes is a constant, focused, urgent commitment to follow that apology with genuine and heartfelt change.

Whether he forgives me or not, I am now, finally, strong, available, present and open. I am now, later than I'd wanted, ready to be his father and I believe in him and his ability to set fire to the world in the best possible way. I am fiercely, unremittingly, devastatingly proud of him.

Bruckner Symphony No. 7, Second Movement
Herbert von Karajan, Conductor

*On one of my first trips to Verona to study with an Italian piano teacher
called Edo, he mentioned the composer Anton Bruckner.*

*'Pile of shit,' I said. 'Overlong pieces, wrote nothing for the piano, boring
and not worth wasting time on.'*

In truth, I'd never heard anything written by him.

*Edo literally slapped me. He sat me down, said to me, 'You do not move
now', and put on a CD of Bruckner's Seventh Symphony. All seventy minutes
of it.*

I didn't move. I couldn't move. It changed me irrevocably.

*Bruckner was a deeply devout Christian (sample quote: 'They want me to
write differently. Certainly I could, but I must not. God has chosen me from
thousands and given me, of all people, this talent. It is to Him that I must
give account. How then would I stand there before Almighty God, if I followed
the others and not Him?') who was short, overweight, lacking social graces*

and hopelessly romantic to the point where he proposed several times to hot young women but was always turned down. He never married, developed severe OCD that resulted in a crippling obsession with numbers, constantly reworked his compositions because he was so self-critical, and drank too much.

He also composed some of the greatest symphonies known to man. Giant, sixty-, seventy-minute and even longer orchestral universes that are the great mountains of musical history.

The Seventh Symphony has four movements, and each one of these epic musical landscapes deserves its own chapter in this book. But it will always be the huge, desperate, second movement that knocks me to the floor like a Tyson left hook.

WHEN I BECAME A FATHER the echoes of my past became screams. There was a cold, insidious certainty growing like a cancer in my entire being that terrible things were going to happen to the most precious thing in my life. It was the single most terrifying thing that I had ever experienced. Everywhere I looked, I could only see danger.

I didn't know it was possible to feel so many powerful emotions at the same time – pure, unadulterated, instantaneous, fat love coupled with a terror so blinding and penetrating I could barely breathe. And there I was, handed this unutterably perfect thing. Those blissfully ignorant nurses might as well have given the keys to an Aston Martin to a four-year-old in Times Square and said, 'Go crazy.'

I insisted on doing the middle-of-the-night feeds. I was up anyway. Anxious, over-thinking, running through all the myriad ways in which he could die at any moment. Knowing at a primal level that something terrible was going to happen to him and that it was only a question of when, not if. Because that is what happens to children.

The plus side is that he and I bonded intensely. I mean, yeah, it's unhealthy, but I lived and breathed him in, twenty-four hours a day. I could not get enough of him. To this day, the happiest, most profoundly peaceful moments of my life have been holding him, fast asleep, a satisfying weight in my arms, feeding him as he slept. I didn't even know you could feed babies while they sleep. Knowing I was nourishing him, protecting him, that at this moment nothing could happen to him.

In the furious, ultra-competitive 'school stakes' of middle-class London, we got him down for a bunch of primary schools, years ahead of schedule. And in every interview with the schools my questions didn't even touch on the facilities, syllabus, food etc.

We'd be sitting in the head teacher's office complete with appalling, frankly lazy children's paintings littering the walls, and she'd be telling us how:

'Our school is an excellent feeder school into the more successful secondary schools in London, with many of our students then going on to the most renowned schools and universities in the country. We have a full and imaginative curriculum, superb facilities, regular field trips, consistently excellent Ofsted reports and a staff-to-student ratio of 1 to 5. We have a major focus not just on academic excellence but believe in meditation, pastoral care and self-development through teamwork and kindness', etc etc.

And I'd sit there, pale and alert, saying:

'Do you hire any male teachers? How many? Are they ever alone with any of the children? What do your police checks entail? Do you have CCTV? In the toilets too? Who takes the children to the toilets? Are they alone? Are any areas of the school not covered by CCTV? How thorough are your background checks? Do you check references thoroughly? Do you monitor the children for symptoms of unhappiness and abuse? What's the school's official procedure if abuse is suspected? Is it written down? May I have a copy?'

I became more and more walking dead. I had to return to work in the City after a few weeks and would leave him at 7 a.m., sobbing in the car as I drove through the dark London streets. I knew what had happened to me just for being a child. It seemed inevitable that similar things would happen to him. That was what childhood was – a war zone filled with danger, threat, terror and pain.

And, simply by bringing him into this world, I felt as if I had hurled him straight into that situation.

And what do you do with that level of guilt? How do you not just drown in it? More to the point, how do you not throw yourself willingly off the tallest building you can find, all the while sneering at what an inexorable heap of shit you are?

And so that's where my façade started to crumble. That moment – what should, could have been the single happiest moment of my life – was the starting point of my descent into a kind of madness I could never have imagined.

I am saying only this: I was raped as a child. Over the course of five years I had sex with a man three times my size and thirty to forty years older than me against my will, painfully, secretively, viciously, dozens and dozens of times. I was turned into a thing to be used. And pain – physical, mental and spiritual – I could handle. But what they don't tell you is that those ripples reach out their cold toxic hands beyond the self. They install an unshakeable belief that all children suffer through childhood in the most abominable ways and that nothing and no one can protect them from it. Just by bringing Jack into this world I had now been complicit in whatever future pain he would surely suffer. The FUCK who did me had not only ruined me, but by proxy he was now going to steal my son's childhood away from him. And that was my fault. And that pain I could not handle. He took my childhood away from me. He took my child away from me. He took fatherhood away from me. And he laughed while he did it. And *that*, disregarding the privilege, the self-obsession, the poncey north London wankiness of my life, you should feel horrified by.

I started to withdraw more and more. The punishing, the passive-aggression, the shaming, mocking, wheedling, judging bullshit that formed almost everything that came out of my mouth descended on my marriage without respite. The fact that Jane stayed with me as long as she did is testament only to her vast reserves of patience and kindness. It does not matter that fundamentally I couldn't love her in 'the right way'. We were a family unit. We had the tools necessary to build a strong, stable, supportive nest for our cub. And rather than wake up and grasp that with every fibre of my being, I pissed all over it.

The selfishness of the victim is the hardest thing to tolerate and treat with compassion. We are idiots. It is nigh on impossible to love us. We push and we push until finally we get what we want – more victimhood. Sometimes my capacity for tolerating and desiring pain is infinite, a bottomless pit of self-hurt and a perverse thrill in seeking more and more.

I guess I could look at this a slightly different way. That my son being born was the beginning of the end of my old life and the start of a new, much more fulfilling life. And in hindsight, that makes perfect sense and would make Deepak Chopra fiercely proud. But spending so many years walking through quicksand, fighting imaginary fires, feeling a never-ending sense of dread and despair, takes its toll.

Things started to happen to me that baffled me because I hadn't experienced them for years and years; I'd cry for no reason, find sleep either impossible or the *only* possible thing I could do. The scariest thing would be losing time – just checking out, without being aware I was doing so, and come back a while later, be it minutes or hours, with no memory of what had happened. My childhood tics started coming back – squeaking, twitching, tapping, light-switch-clicking – and I lost my appetite for everything from food to sex to TV. The lights were going out and I had no clue why or how to stop it.

So I looked for distractions. I looked for a way out that didn't involve homicide or suicide. And all roads led to music. They always do. I couldn't be a musician, I knew that after ten years without playing a single note on the piano that was not an option, but perhaps I could become an agent. Anything that got me out of the City and even vaguely towards music had to be a step in the right direction. And so I did what an egocentric City-working cock would do – found the address for the agent who represented the greatest pianist in the world and set about forming a business partnership with him.

It wasn't hard. A case of Krug, a few emails, a meal or two and I was set. His name was Franco. He lived in Verona. He had looked after my hero, Grigory Sokolov, for twenty years. Grigory Sokolov – without question, the greatest living pianist. Arguably the greatest pianist of all time. A man who managed again and again and again to use the notes of a piano to reach into your soul, rip out whatever was in there, shake it about, polish it, take it for a ride and then put it back again in a way that just fit a bit better. This guy, this weird, autistic savant. This chubby, awkward, introverted statesman of the piano, had been my musical crack for a decade since I'd heard his first album. It was all Chopin. And live. Most live albums (my own included) are cobbled together from at least two performances; the producers and engineers take all the best bits and merge them together into one 'live' album. If the label is feeling especially cheeky, they also go into the studio post-concert and cover any dodgy bits, a process known as patching, and make sure they don't mention it anywhere. It's a blatant misrepresentation, but we do it because we're needy and insecure and cannot bear the thought of offering something that is less than perfect. But not Sokolov. One concert, one take, some cold, coughing Russians in the audience and the most visceral, staggering performance of Chopin's Second Sonata and Op. 25 études I'd ever heard. It's on iTunes – don't just take my word for it.

There began a love affair, made even more tantalising given he has only released a tiny handful of albums. The rest were gathered online, child-porn style, via developmentally disabled pianophiles (it's a real word, I promise) and listened to in total awe.

So the thought of working with his agent, who had brought him over to the West from Russia as a young man and turned him into a phenomenon, performing to sold-out audiences all around the world, was overwhelmingly exciting.

With Jane's blessing, I quit my job, my excitement just about countering the slight feeling of nausea at walking away from such a reliable income, and Franco and I decided we'd both chuck in €30,000 and open a London office. But before doing that we agreed I should go to Verona for a couple of weeks and learn the ropes. Which I did. Eagerly.

Franco lives in the only high-rise building in Verona, towering above the city with the most extraordinary views, floor-to-ceiling windows, a €1,000 coffee machine and a Yamaha grand piano. That, right there, is all you need in this world. And after dinner on my first night he asked me if I played the piano. I mumbled something about not having played for years but that I used to play well enough for a teenager. So he asked if I'd play him something. And I, being hungry for approval and attention and a bit high from the pasta and views and Italian-city smell, sat at the piano and somehow whacked out a piece by Chopin. It was, to my ears, messy and embarrassing. But I'd remembered all of it, got through it and, a little bit red in the face, turned around afterwards to see his reaction. He was sat there, jaw on the floor and totally silent. And after a minute he simply said to me:

'James, I have been doing this for twenty-five years and I have never heard someone play the piano like that who was not a professional pianist. You are not going to become an agent. You will come every month here to Verona, stay with me, and study with my friend Edo who is the best teacher in all of Italy. You may not become successful, but you have to try.'

And that was that.

He then spent the next few days dragging me round to all of his friends' houses (all of whom had pianos) and forcing me to play to them like some kind of newly trained puppy. And it was weird and wonderful and scarcely believable to me. After a decade of not playing and trying to make peace with the fact that I would never be able to do what I'd always dreamed of, Franco had thrown a hand grenade into the equation.

And one morning we ended up at Edo's house. And this was one of the guys who really changed my life forever. The most violent, aggressive, arrogant, dictatorial bastard I'd ever met. The perfect teacher for someone like me who was lazy, ill-disciplined, badly trained and overly enthusiastic. I had my first lesson with him that day. We walked together to the music shop and bought a Mozart sonata (the F major one, for those who care). Which was a shit start because (a) I hated Mozart (in much the same adolescent way I hated everything I didn't know or understand, because I was too small-minded and lazy to get to know him better), and (b) I thought we should start with a massive, showy Rachmaninov concerto.

And then we got to work. In a way I had never known existed. Slowly, carefully, with an almost inhuman attention to detail, intense concentration, a ton of pencilling. He showed me tricks that made everything possible, the most useful being his rhythm method; most tricky passages in piano-playing involve runs of fast notes. And he broke down those runs into groups of either four or three notes at a time. And then further broke them down into different rhythms – ten in total, each one putting emphasis on a different one of that group either by accenting it, or dotting the note before (holding it down 50 per cent longer than marked). It was a bit like a long-distance runner breaking down each and every mechanical movement he's asking his body to do while running a marathon and then practising each micro-movement again and again one after the other until he starts to put them all together.

I'd train my fingers to play every variation of every group of notes in every possible way and then play the whole passage through, and fuck me if the fiftieth time through I didn't play it perfectly as written. It was like a door opening: spend a few hours working methodically and slowly and you will end up playing brilliantly much, much more quickly and reliably than just going at it with a sledgehammer approach. It was a huge revelation, because what it meant was that all the pieces I'd thought impossible to play suddenly became possible. I finally understood the 0.2 of a second rule that Edo had told me about – the idea that to most people, that length of time is just a blink of an eye, but to a Formula One driver it is the difference between coming first and coming tenth. Most people can get good enough at the piano in a relatively short period of time, but to get to the top, to up your game by the 0.2 of a second required to move from good to great, can take twenty-five years of this kind of relentless, concentrated, consistent work. I felt like someone who'd been paralysed from the waist down and was suddenly able to walk again, albeit with a lot of hard work and training.

And so that is what I did. Hard work and training. Every month I would fly over from Gatwick to Verona, spend four days with Edo and then go back home to practise. It was in equal parts soul-destroying and exhilarating. He was so nasty, so critical, so hyper-controlling – often I'd see a mobile phone winging its way towards me from the corner of my eye as he hurled it at me in disgust, or had him screaming at me, spittle flying out of his mouth, raging at me in Italian. On the (very rare) occasion I played in a way he found acceptable he would simply shrug and say, 'What's next?' My piano scores are still filled with his writing – delightful acronyms like DWTFYW ('do what the fuck you want', to be heard in his exasperated, disappointed, surly tone), BABY KILLER (expressing disapproval over an interpretive approach of mine), and the simple, if accurate, SHIT. But I didn't really care because I was playing pieces I had been in awe of my whole life – Chopin's Third Sonata and Second Piano Concerto, Beethoven's 'Waldstein' Sonata and Op. 109 sonata, Bach's Partitas, giant Chopin pieces like the Polonaise-Fantasie and F minor Fantasie, Rachmaninov études, Liszt's Hungarian Rhapsodies.

We even bought a new piano, the most beautiful Steinway Model B. And for what it's worth, Steinway truly are the best pianos in the world. There simply is no competition. And their prices reflect it – I increased our mortgage to buy the piano (a vomit-inducing £55,000) and it sat in our front room, the most profoundly valuable thing I'd ever owned.

I would spend hours each day practising – and practising correctly, too; slowly, methodically, intelligently, before treating myself by playing through the whole piece and seeing people walking by outside stop and take a few minutes to stand still and listen (I would close the shutters out of embarrassment but still peek through and see them there). We had a nanny who looked after Jack for a few hours each day while I practised, and then we would spend time as a family cooking, walking, playing, hanging out. It felt almost believable. The noise in my head had receded, replaced with notes and music, and it seemed to allow me some space to function more effectively. Life was a bit less fragile and a little softer and easier. It seemed manageable.

And Jack was still being a miracle, learning to walk, talk, laugh and grab. Still the most beautiful thing I'd ever seen in my life. I, from the outside at least, had it all: a pretty, supportive, successful wife and perfect child, a lovely 2,000-square-foot home with a giant garden and brand new Steinway, time and space to pursue my dream career, plenty of money in the bank, lush car, good friends – it was the ostensibly complete life.

There are many things I wish for. Cricket matches to not be able to last five days and still end in a draw. A massive increase in awareness and funding for mental health units and rape crisis centres. A six pack. KFC to deliver.

But most of all, I wish I could settle for what things looked like rather than what they felt like. I wish I could just have looked at my life then and said, 'Yep. Nailed it. Settle in, relax and enjoy.' How much easier things would be without my head. It should have been obvious that symptomatic relief brought about by a change in career, as with any new miracle fix, be it a new girl, a bit more money, a new house or a fucking holiday, is invariably temporary. It quickly becomes harder and harder to convince the self that things are different, and before long my previously silent brain companions started coming back to the foreground in my head and letting me know how fucked I was.

The unease that I had felt when my son was born returned and I started to feel this cold hand of something grimy and slimy crawling up the back of my neck. This fucking thing that just would not leave me alone no matter how hard I tried to move away from it. This giant, filthy come-stain that had been following me around like a malicious stray pit bull for decades.

Once again the piano started to turn on me, the lustre of learning these magnificent new pieces started to fade, replaced with constant self-criticism at my inability to play them perfectly. I was getting more and more frustrated, starting to spin out quicker and quicker day by day, like someone had turned on a slow-boiling kettle in my stomach and mind that was gradually getting hotter and hotter. I wasn't sure what had happened or why, but I knew something wasn't right.

And functioning as an adult, husband, father, civilised human being while all this was happening was something of a challenge. I carried on, on autopilot, for as long as I could, but I was fighting a losing battle and I knew it. It was a question of when – and not if – all hell would break loose.

Ironically, it started when I asked for help for the first time. It was getting more and more apparent that I was unable to function the way I wanted to, or the way my family needed me to. I'd successfully kept my wife out of the loop for a long time – not hard to do when there are changes of career, work deadlines, new houses and a toddler thrown into the mix. I had, in the past, made a couple of oblique references to abuse in front of her, but it had never been discussed or properly acknowledged. Whatever honest version of love had been there in the beginning had either disappeared completely or (more likely) was buried under the weight of denial, relentless point-scoring and my own self-obsession.

I could deal with suffering, but eventually I couldn't deal with my family paying the price for it. And one day, looking online, I found a reference to a charity that focused on helping male survivors of sexual assault. I'm not sure why, but I called them. Maybe it was boredom, maybe I was sick and tired of being sick and tired. Maybe it was a final, desperate attempt to see if anything could be salvaged or made bearable.

They were based in London Bridge and offered me a confidential appointment the next day. And the big question, still, is 'Had I known what would unravel, would I still have gone?' Probably not.

I arrived (two hours early, as normal) and eventually was shown in to a standard 'shrink's office by Ikea' room – two comfortable but not too comfortable chairs, a low coffee table between them, Kleenex in the middle, muted tones, wanky seascapes on the walls. A woman with the loveliest face imaginable was there. Open, kind, totally loving and non-judgmental. And, for all my resolve to dance around the subject, to not talk about anything too personal, keep the walls up, it all came out. Thirty years of it just poured out of me from start to finish. Everything in as much detail as I could remember. I didn't make eye contact once, but just went at it like an actor auditioning for the role of 'autistic, lunatic, ashamed rape victim'. And the only thing I remember her saying to me afterwards was, 'Have you told your wife?' Which was as alien a concept to me as suggesting I start training to walk on the moon.

'Of course I haven't told my wife!'

<Disbelief>

'Why not?'

'What the fuck! Why the fuck would I tell my wife?'

'Because she's your wife. This has all started to come out now and the road is going to get trickier and narrower, and you're going to need as much support as possible.'

<Incomprehensible stare>

That's another thing they don't tell you. Once you start talking you're fucked. The perpetrators who swear you to secrecy were right all along. You can't put it back in the box. It's like lancing a boil, except what comes out is a seemingly endless jet of pus, bile, toxic waste that does not diminish or lessen but rather increases in intensity and volume until you are fucking drowning in it.

'You need to tell her. You need to tell her today. You need to ask her for some help.'

I had told a stranger, with guaranteed confidentiality (I had asked about that at least twelve times to confirm it), and not given my real name or mentioned any identifiable names of schools or teachers. And now, apparently, I had to tell my wife things that I had spent my entire life locked in and hidden away.

And the thing is that I knew she was right. Not because I felt I needed support, but because this thing was out of its box now, and just like bungee-jumping off a cliff, once you leave the edge there is no going back. I was in freefall, and Jane was, potentially, my parachute, and I knew, just absolutely knew, that now it was out there in the atmosphere I was in real danger. If you spend long enough thinking you will die if you tell your secrets, then you end up believing it. If a rapist tells a five-year-old child again and again what monstrous things will happen to him if he ever tells anyone, it is assimilated, unquestioned, accepted as absolute truth. And I'd told someone and the clock was now ticking and time was running out and I was more fucked than I'd ever thought possible. To all intents and purposes I was now a five-year-old masquerading as a thirty-one-year-old, with no defence, no skills at dissimulation I could fall back on, no way out but through.

I texted my wife and asked her to meet me for dinner that night at a restaurant we both loved. I got there feeling clammy, sick, just ill with fuckedness. Because I knew that what I was going to tell her would eventually destroy us once and for all and that she was in no way equipped to give me what I needed. I didn't even know what I needed. So I felt like a suicide bomber with a backpack full of C-4, about to blow up a bunch of innocents and unable to back out. Relax, I know it's not the same thing. But feelings sometimes feel like Auschwitz, even if in reality they're closer to Butlins. Real compassion comes from understanding that what feels true for someone is, to all intents and purposes, true. Doesn't matter a bit if it is patently untrue to you and everyone else. And this terror felt true to me. It was my reality, however skewed that may seem.

She knew something was up. I looked dreadful and couldn't meet her eye. And so when she asked me what was wrong I just laid it out for her. Cold, clipped, matter of fact. And I knew there and then we were done. That this fucking guy had ruined me and, twenty-five years on, my marriage too.

The important thing to mention is that my wife was, is, the love-liest woman. She is capable of stupefying levels of kindness and compassion. And I know that it was a case of 'couldn't' not 'wouldn't'. She literally could not respond in a way that was going to help salvage things. It was like trying to put a body back together after it had jumped on a hand grenade. With all the willingness in the world, it just ain't going to happen. We left the restaurant and drove home in silence. And I sat in my son's room, looking at his four-year-old little body. And just fucking cried.

Liszt, 'Totentanz'
Sergio Tiempo, Piano

Liszt is the wanker who is responsible for making pianists perform full-length piano recitals from memory. This was never done before — concerts were a mixture of different musicians and genres of music, and performers always used the score. And then this nineteenth-century rock star, the Paganini of the piano and Keith Richards of his day, shattered performance convention by giving long, memorised piano recitals, and playing faster, louder, harder and more violently than anyone had ever done before. He composed treacherous, monumentally difficult pieces for piano: transcriptions of all the Beethoven symphonies for solo piano, virtuoso showpieces based on popular operatic themes of the day, dozens of études which remain almost impossible to perform accurately unless you're a fucking machine.

A child prodigy who quickly morphed into a womanising, super-rich showman, it all got a bit much for him, and several affairs and children later he took holy orders at the age of forty-six and joined a Franciscan order, continuing to play and compose until his death in 1886 at the age of seventy-five.

In addition to two piano concertos, he wrote a few pieces for piano and orchestra, one of which was called the 'Dance of Death'. He was slightly obsessed with death, frequenting Parisian hospitals and asylums and even prison dungeons to see those who had been condemned to die. Many of his works have titles linked with the same subject, and this piece, this overwhelmingly terrifying seventeen minutes of piano fury is based on the famous Dies Irae — *the death theme used by composers from Rachmaninov to Berlioz.*

This performance is a live one by Sergio Tiempo and I genuinely have yet to hear a performance so ridiculously bombastic. The guy just has two incredible hands, zero fear and an absolute conviction of what he wants to say. It's astonishing.

HINDSIGHT IS CRYSTAL CLEAR. I can see now that I had let a very old, very toxic secret out. I had brought my wife into it (without her consent — she had ostensibly married a decent, undamaged, stand-up guy), I had embarked on a ridiculously ambitious career change, and my son had just turned four. What the fuck did I think was going to happen?

Here's another heads-up for victims of abuse. It is, apparently, very common for the world to spin completely off its axis when your child approaches the age you were when the abuse began. I didn't know this. My psyche did. I was blindsided. There was something inside me, clawing at me, desperate to get out, and I just could not keep it in any longer. It felt like my mind was a computer that had been pushed too hard for too long and simply exploded. My brain literally felt hot. It's the weirdest feeling; not pleasant, overwhelmingly scary. And I was scrabbling around for anything that would fix it, however temporary.

I knew drink and drugs were an option. I also knew that if I went down that route I would end up dead (fair enough) but more importantly I'd probably destroy the people I loved most too.

And then, just as I was desperate to find something that was halfway between suicide and murder, I found razor blades.

I'd done what any self-respecting guy in my situation would have done and gone online looking for solutions to what was happening. And I'd found the glorious, unhinged world of the online forum. Anonymous, intonation-free, text-based cesspits masquerading as help but merely a front for vomiting all of the various neuroses, perversions, kinks and foibles out into the world in the hope of ending the feeling of 'always alone' and possibly finding someone worse than you. And on one of these sites people were talking about cutting. As if it were a bad thing – how they'd done it again but were furious about doing so and wished they could stop. It was something I'd heard about, usually in connection with teenage girls, but it had never occurred to me to do it myself.

But everything hurt, and it seemed like a good idea at the time. And so in the most banal way imaginable, I popped off down to the local chemist and bought a five-pack of Wilkinson Sword razor blades and some bandages.

This part of the book is likely to trigger the fuck out of anyone with similar issues. So skip it or call a friend. And before you judge me too much for what I'm about to share, perhaps a few words about the act of carving your arms up.

Self-harm (SH from here on in) is a wonder drug. It is reaching pandemic levels in the UK, where we already have the highest rate of SH in Europe. Instead of tapas and siestas we are reaching for small metallic objects with sharp edges and strips of absorbent material. And the reason for this is that it is the most effective, immediate and electric high, one that is only equalled by heroin (injecting not smoking) and crack cocaine. It has no come down, no negative side effects (when done right), costs next to nothing, can be done anywhere and you only ever need to score from Boots (or your kitchen drawer if they're closed).

It involves all the 'safe' elements that make illegal drugs so appealing (ritual, thought control, feelings slam, isolation, escape, general 'fuck the world' rage) and adds in a dose of visceral self-hatred, immunity from arrest (unless you're very unlucky), greater control, a healthy(ish) expression of rage and the lovely feeling of being able to scream out to the world about how much pain you're in without having to say it out loud. Remember that feeling of wanting to tell on someone at school who was bullying you/abusing you, but not feeling able to? Magnify that by a million and then imagine you could go back in time, set fire to that person again and again, force them to watch you decapitate their family and then do a jig in front of them as they burn slowly to death. You can achieve all of that and then some with a £1 box of Wilkinson Sword blades and a 20p bandage.

And that is why wanting to stop it and seeing it as a bad thing is a losing battle. Something like this can never, will never, be dealt with by talking, mental health charity adverts, waiting room leaflets and well-meaning teachers. It works too well, the pay-off is too great, the endorphin release too intense.

It is a regular, consistent, effective coping mechanism. And it is as rife as the not-so-hidden Valium craze of the 1970s. The majority of those who engage in this behaviour are catastrophically misunderstood, misdiagnosed, mistreated. SH is *not* an indicator of suicidal ideation. It is *not* indicative of a threat to others. It does *not* mean that you are less capable of functioning well. Russell Brand, Johnny Depp, Colin Farrell, Alfred Kinsey, Sid Vicious are a few high-profile men who have used it. The list of women is far longer.

This is not something done only by skinny teenage girls (although far too many of them indulge frequently). It is invariably a response to a culture in which we rush around invisible and unheard and find ourselves unable to keep up with the pace and stresses of modern life. A place where, male or female, we must parent, earn and achieve in unsustainable and impossibly increasing ways. And even if we manage to get to that place of achievement, the surprise is that it makes not the slightest bit of difference. We still feel shabby and less-than.

But that day I found a cure, a way to stop feeling quite so shit about myself.

I get home to an empty flat. Jack is out with Jane. I'm shaking as I set out the little cutting kit on the bathroom floor, sat cross-legged. I stare at my arms and decide which one and where. I figure left forearm is the place to start. So I pull off my T-shirt, take out and unwrap a single blade. It is impossibly shiny and kind of scary to look at – smooth, flexible, tiny, ludicrously sharp. I push it down into the skin and then angle it upwards and inwards and drag it hard across about an inch of flesh, pushing down as I do so. At first nothing at all. No pain, no nothing. And then about a second or two later, I see the skin literally open up, blood appearing magically, pain rushing through my body, the flesh opening. And the blood keeps coming. Far more than I'd thought. I had totally miscalculated the pressure needed. Bandages were going to do fuck all so I grabbed a towel and used that. I was starting to panic – there was blood all over the white, tiled floor, the towel was getting soaked through, I couldn't enjoy my high at all. I had completely screwed this up.

I called my best friend Matthew because he and his wife were a kind of medical power-couple – he a psychologist, she the head of ER at a hospital ten minutes' drive from my house. And of course he came round, drove me to his wife's hospital, had a quiet word with her, helpfully avoiding a psych consult and the long, drunken queue of miserable bastards already there, and she kindly, gently, flushed it, stitched it, bandaged it and let me out.

I played every card in the book to keep them quiet. To not interrogate me, call my wife, come home with me, confiscate my blades. To convince them it was my first time and wouldn't happen ever again, that I was horrified and had made a terrible mistake. And of course that's what good friends do, isn't it? They left me, mercifully, to my own devices, and went on with their business. And I got home, cleaned up the floor and tried again. A little less pressure, a little more attention to detail. And this time it was perfect. Three inch-long slices, not deep enough to require stitches, not shallow enough to allow the pain to subside too quickly. Just right. And it felt like a heroin high. Only cleaner. That feeling of falling back down onto the bathroom floor, satisfied, spent, exhilarated was everything I'd hoped it would be and more.

That's the thing about cutting – not only do you get high, but you can express your disgust at yourself and the world, control the pain yourself, enjoy the ritual, the endorphins, the seedy, gritty, self-violence privately and hurt no one other than yourself. It felt like having a particularly seedy sexual affair, whilst saving a fortune on hotel rooms and not having to betray your wife and forensically scrub cell phones and email inboxes.

And it did its job well. I'd found something, albeit temporary, that helped me function better, be more available, show up for my family, put on the mask. It became a kind of dirty, daily reprieve from falling apart, and gave me just enough strength to act like a husband and father to the outside world, but not quite enough to remove the stink of weird, not-quite-rightness surrounding me while I did it.

I'd play my piano having dropped Jack at nursery school, break between practice sessions to cut myself, pick him up at the end of the day and we'd all spend the evening as a family doing what families do. It was schizophrenic and weird and wrong but I couldn't get out of it.

There is this peculiar twist inside me that forbids me to enjoy things that I like unless they are hidden. With the sole exception of smoking, everything that is pleasurable brings shame. Sex – secretive and hidden away with the lights off. Piano – shutters down, door closed, never in front of other people unless they've paid for tickets. Drugs – alone in a shabby room undisturbed. Cutting – behind a locked bathroom door. Eating – usually quickly and urgently in the kitchen, away from prying eyes. Spending money on nice things – hidden from my wife, done online away from shop assistants, delivered anonymously via the mail by a judgmental postman. Holding my son – in the dead of night as the world slept, alone in his room, his breathing deafening me.

Life is temporary, dangerous, hostile and aggressive. And I acted accordingly. I should have got out of it then and there. Made my apologies, filed for divorce, surgically removed myself from the equation, fled the country, started afresh somewhere far away where I might have been able to buy a few more years of relative peace. But I didn't. Instead, I decided to organise my first public concert.

It was an outstanding idea. Just as things are beginning to fall apart, when there is pressure coming from every angle – pressure to make the marriage work, to be the best father on the planet, to play the piano like a genius, to be a man – I decide to add to it by giving my first performance. To show those closest to me and myself that I wasn't a total waste of space, and that the work I'd been doing was actually bearing fruit.

I found a concert hall to rent on London's South Bank that had about 400 seats and was a stone's throw away from the Festival Hall. I found a children's charity that I could align it with (so as to avoid the arrogance of charging money to see me play and also pretend I was doing something vaguely noble and altruistic). And I set the date for a few weeks' time.

I was playing a stupendous programme – three giant pieces by Bach, Beethoven and Chopin (the holy trinity of piano music), perhaps 120,000 notes, all from memory, all with the right fingering, all with the right touch, pedal, nuance, all the time being aware of the note that came before and the note that comes after, all merged into one glorious whole and sent out of the piano to a waiting audience. It's a hell of a thing to do, especially for the first time. Most pianists – well, all pianists – have been doing that since the age of nine or ten, younger in Asia. I had just turned thirty-one. I had no idea about nerves, performance practice, breathing, how to deal with audience noise and how to concentrate for two hours to such a degree. I could barely make it through an episode of *EastEnders* without (literally) losing the plot.

The hall was rammed. I've no idea why. Friends came, friends of friends came, the hall must have emailed their database because there were also strangers, music lovers, randoms, hundreds of people crammed in, last-minute scrabbles to find extra chairs, me backstage wanting to vom, lights down, last coughs, that unique noise heard in concert halls all over the world as the audience settles into the expectation of something beneath words. And on I walk.

Shrinks talk a lot about finding a safe place. Somewhere that you can go to in your head that engenders a feeling of well-being and relaxation. Perhaps the nook of someone's arm, a favourite beach, a childhood bedroom. I know now that mine, invariably, is sat in front of a grand piano, single spotlight on the keys, the rest of the room in total darkness. All I can see in my field of vision is a black and white keyboard with eighty-eight keys and, preferably, the gold letters that spell out 'Steinway'.

And thank fuck for that. Because after walking on trembling, I sit on the stool and something takes over. I disappear in a good way. Without flying out of my body, without searing pain in my ass, without tears and blood and concrete boots. It is the best thing ever, like having a four-handed, naked, hot stone Bach massage. Everything goes by in a flash and, at the same time, the world seems to slow right down and all of my anxieties about time disappear. There is infinite space in between the notes, total awe at the sound my fingers are producing (not the quality, simply the fact that I am somehow doing this), a sense of coming home. This must be what Sting was talking about when he was raving about tantric sex.

It goes well. A few fluffed notes, no major memory lapses (I still have a recording of it), decent voicing (where the melody sings out properly), new (to me) musical interpretations of pieces that have been played for centuries. And I realise that all of those fantasies about giving concerts that I had as a kid, that kept me alive and safe in my head, were accurate. It really is that powerful. And I knew I wanted to do it forever. No matter what.

We had a big dinner afterwards to celebrate. I was treated kindly. Even Edo, who had flown over from Italy, was complimentary. My wife brought me flowers. We ate all the dim sum. My adrenaline levels had spiked, crashed, done cartwheels. I didn't sleep that night. Now, a few years down the line and after a couple of hundred concerts, this has become almost normalised for me. But then? It was like having sex for the first time with someone who was your spiritual twin. And hotter than hot. A bigger high than heroin and cutting and everything else destructive. It was my own personal, private nirvana.

And for a few weeks, it stayed with me. I was still cutting regularly and hiding it from Jane (long-sleeved T-shirts helped). I was still wrestling with voices in my head I didn't understand or want. But I was functioning well enough. And I was still enjoying some kind of afterglow from giving my first concert. I'd had a taste of something that felt immortal. Looking back, those few weeks post-concert seemed to be like walking on a tightrope while largely oblivious to the circling sharks underneath waiting for me to fall off. My life revolved around my son, my piano, my razor blades and doing my utmost to convince my wife and the rest of the world that everything was OK.

I did a pretty decent job of not thinking too much about things (harder than it sounds) and threw myself into other endeavours. And for a short time, cutting aside, it felt like we had a chance.

I don't think I shall ever understand what happened next. On paper it seems like this was the perfect springboard into a new career. I could have found an agent, given more concerts, forged my way in this weird, wonderful musical world. Carved a little niche just for me. My life could have been a succession of concerts, practising, hanging out with Jack, working on my marriage. That would have been lovely. Normal and extraordinary at once. I could have put down the razor blades, found a decent shrink to work through some of the bigger mind-bombs, put one foot in front of the other day by day and moved gently towards a good life.

Nothing, absolutely nothing, was stopping me from doing that. Again, this is why it is so hard to have patience with people like me. In front of me are two doors. One clearly labelled 'Good Life', the other 'Hell'. And not only did I walk into the dark one, but I did so whistling, all nonchalant, rolling my sleeves up purposefully. I strutted like the biggest cock in the world into Arma-fucking-geddon.

Brahms, 'German Requiem', First Movement
Herbert von Karajan, Conductor

Brahms was both traditionalist and innovator when it came to composing. He was a leading light of the Austrian musical scene but didn't get involved in the War of the Romantics between composers such as Liszt and Wagner, who represented a more radical approach to composition, preferring to stick to a more conservative route. One of the holy trinity of Bs (along with Bach and Beethoven), he remains one of the great musical grandfathers of our time, with his symphonies, piano concertos, chamber music and piano compositions a consistent part of the mainstream repertoire.

As a kid his family was so broke he was forced to play the piano in 'dance halls' (read 'brothels') to earn money, and possibly because of some dodgy experiences that occurred at that time he remained unable to form any real, functional relationships with women as he grew up. He did, however, have a massive boner for Schumann's wife Clara. The fact that immediately after her husband Robert's death Brahms rushed to be with her and that they both destroyed numerous personal letters to one another seems to imply there was something going on worth hiding.

In 1865 his mother died and, wracked with grief, he wrote his 'German Requiem', which to this day is one of his most celebrated and performed works. It had a slightly inauspicious beginning when the timpanist at its premiere misread the dynamic marking as 'ff' (very loud) rather than 'pp' (very quiet) and drowned out the other musicians, but since then it has become one of his most performed and admired works.

There is something overwhelmingly haunting about religious grief, and this piece of music, like Mozart's and Fauré's requiems deserves its place in music history as the absolute pinnacle of the genre.

MY WIFE PUT HER ARM around me one evening. Normal thing to do. Rather nice, even. That afternoon had been stressful for me and I'd cut. I'd got it down to once or twice a week, but this was a fresh one, and when her hand touched my arm, I flinched. Couldn't help it. She asked me what was wrong, I got flustered, she wouldn't believe me when I said 'nothing', there was the weight of a lie in the air, and she told me (not asked me) to show her my arm. And so I did. I was so tired of hiding stuff from her. I'd remembered back in the day when she and I had first started dating, how kind she had been, how solid we had seemed, how invincible. That couldn't have just disappeared, no matter how big an asshole I appeared to have become.

So I took off my shirt and showed her and, genuinely horrified, she properly lost her shit. I'd carved the word 'toxic' into my upper arm with a razor blade.

I know. Very teenage and melodramatic. But it was how I felt. And razor blade font is awesome. But she thought it was much more serious than I did. I could see her anger, and underneath it love, concern, kindness, fear. She made me promise to go see someone for help, and of course I agreed. She wasn't buying my whole 'it's really not as big a deal as you think' routine. She gave me a deadline of a week, and, another secret out in the open, I began to spiral more and more quickly out of control.

I didn't sleep. Couldn't move. Couldn't eat. Couldn't talk. Properly 'on the bed prostrate, eyes glazed over, head hot, fucked'. And when you're like that you have finally reached the point where you don't care any more. There is simply no deeper level of self-hatred and shame you can go to. You're at the bottom and everything falls apart. It is at once exhilarating, freeing and excruciating. It felt like the link inside me that was holding everything together had just snapped – as if any semblance of doing the right thing, being a decent person, had been swept away in a wave of gigantic indifference.

I seemed to accept that nothing was going to work and had therefore made the decision to kill myself, and with that acceptance came the most amazing sense of liberation.

The best part about wanting to kill yourself is the energy you feel once you've made your decision. It's a bit like being given wings after trudging through quicksand for a few years. Also, the planning involved is extremely fun. It's like making a playlist for someone you love – it needs a lot of thought, you get all excited about what it will end up like and how they will react, you enjoy the process of making it as much as the final product.

I'd figured jumping or hanging was the way to go. And, fuck me, the internet is a big help with this stuff. Swathes of pages about what height to jump from, suitable locations, what to avoid, how best to do it. I even found a 'height to weight' chart for those wanting to hang themselves – it ensures the length of the drop is suitable for the person's weight so that they're not left in a coma or still functioning after they do the deed. Handy.

A friend of mine called me as I was in the midst of planning. Stephen. He was a remarkable guy – left school in a Welsh mining village at fifteen with no qualifications at all and by sixteen was playing to a sold-out Madison Square Garden with a huge British rock band. Twenty years later, covered in tattoos and still without any qualifications, he decides he wants to become a surgeon, enrols in Columbia med school, works his ass off and is now, astonishingly, a fucking surgeon. We'd been extremely close a few years previously until he'd moved to New York and we'd lost touch. He caught me on a bad day. I cracked a joke about finding a building to jump off, tried to backtrack, didn't think I'd successfully convinced him I'd been joking, put the phone down and punched myself in the face. I guess Jane had been in touch with him, asking him to check up on me.

I'm rereading this (should have left it to my editor). And I am so aware of the light this shows me in. It is text-book narcissism and self-pity. I see that now. But when you're in it, feeling like you're drowning in this shit, and everything seems so damn real, you cannot see the whole picture. There is no room for reality with depression, trauma, PTSD, whatever you want to call it. My world had collapsed in on itself and there was room only for me and my delusions and ego. There was no other option than to remove myself from the world; one of the most dangerous misunderstandings about suicide is that to those considering it, it is almost always an absolutely valid choice. It's a bit like being absolutely starving, having not eaten for days, and suddenly being at a restaurant where the only thing they serve is something you absolutely fucking hate and would not in a million years have eaten before, but it's the only possible option. You order it, you eat it, you cram it in your mouth as fast as you can using your hands, you don't stop until you're about to pass out. The reality of my situation as I saw it, together with my raging head, had begun to shake the foundations of my complacency to the point where the element, the luxury, of choice had been removed from me.

There was one possible last-ditch solution that was thrown my way a couple of days before I was going to go through with my plan (my in-laws were due in town from the States and it felt right to wait until they were there so there was at least some support for my wife in the aftermath). I'd gone to an AA meeting, a regular one of mine, and when I got home Jane and my buddy Matthew were there waiting for me. Clearly, Stephen's report of our telephone conversation hadn't been great.

I don't want to talk much about AA because, well, the second A stands for Anonymous. But I will say that in my experience (nineteen years without a drink and still attending regular meetings), it is the easiest and most successful way of stopping drinking. It is a remarkable invention and one that creates miracles day after day, but it is predicated on the fact that there is a certain level of honesty, especially self-honesty, amongst its members. Even that is not necessary all the time; simply having the willingness to stop drinking at some point is enough. But I was going to meetings and chatting to other people there with a degree of fundamental dishonesty that made it impossible for me to get well. I stayed sober physically, but mentally was a different story. And therefore, other than being dry, I was not a well bunny, and missed out on the opportunity to transcend my demons that so many others in AA have managed to do. I do know this though – had I started drinking again I would be dead. There is no doubt in my mind – it is much, much easier to kill yourself drunk than it is sober. And in that respect I owe AA my life. And now, today, with a newfound honesty that can only really come from emerging out of a violently degrading rock bottom, I also owe it my peace of mind. It is the best thing ever.

So I got home from lying my ass off at yet another meeting about how great I was doing, and was greeted, gently, by my wife and best buddy. They told me they had looked into hospitals that dealt specifically with sexual abuse and suggested (as in, 'If you don't go we'll make sure you're put there regardless') I go down the next morning and meet with the intake team. They had no idea that I had already found the building I was going to jump from, had made a will, written a letter with computer passwords, bank account details, burial requests etc. And it put me in a quandary. I could lie to them and, instead of going down to the hospital the next day, I could simply top myself then, or I could do as they asked. I could do as they asked because there was nothing else left, and even if there was a fraction of a percentage chance of finding something helpful that could avoid such a permanent solution, then perhaps it was worth it.

And so after a few hours of them repeatedly reassuring me that Jack would be OK, that they could function perfectly well without me and that my in-laws were in town for a couple of weeks to help pick up the slack, I said OK. And the next morning I drove down to the hospital.

It was a fucking disaster from the start.

I'm not sure how much of this was me being a dick and how much of it was them being unprofessional wankers, but Jesus Christ, this place was horrific. For all their spiel about specific programmes to help deal with sexual abuse trauma there was none of it. A couple of morbidly overweight 'therapists', a sulky group of heroin addicts sent there against their will by a well-meaning NHS, a psychiatrist who could barely speak English and a bunch of rules enforced with all the glee of a bullied red-headed stepchild finally able to exact revenge on his tormentors.

Any time I opened my mouth to ask a question or see if I could speak to someone higher up in the team I was told to shut up, boot-camp style, and accused of being a troublemaker. I lasted forty-eight hours before deciding it wasn't for me. I'd hidden a pack of razor blades when I'd arrived out in the back garden, which I retrieved and used to cut yet again. Even that didn't do it for me. And so I packed my bags and asked them for my mobile phone, car keys and wallet (confiscated on arrival) as I was leaving. And they said no. Just like that.

I laughed a bit and then said, 'Seriously, I need my stuff back and then I'll be out of your hair.'

And then they said they'd discuss it and I should come to the office in a couple of hours.

So I wander round the place for a bit and just before lunchtime in I go. There in front of me are a bunch of people I've never seen before.

Doctors, nurses and a few others, all looking severe and vaguely threatening. I giggle and crack a joke about this being some kind of intervention. Nothing. Stony silence.

It was like some low-budget TV court scene. They had searched my room and found the packet of razor blades ('I never leave home without them' not an adequate defence apparently); they told me that the consensus amongst staff and clients ('patients' was not adequately PC) was that I was a negative influence; they told me they deemed me a danger to myself or others as a result of this and that they were going to send me to another hospital where I could be 'more appropriately looked after'. And just like that, the walls came tumbling down.

The removal of choice is one of the greatest terrors you can inflict on someone. From the age of ten, when I left the school where the abuse was happening, I had always had a choice. I could have told someone, I could have been less promiscuous, I could have asked for help, stayed single, pursued the piano, said no to drugs and on and on. I chose to not do all of those things. I even chose, eventually, to ask for help. And now, for the first time since I was five years old and face down on a gym mat, squashed under the weight of a giant, I once again had no choice. I couldn't talk my way out of this (though I tried), I couldn't fight my way out of it (again, I tried, despite a couple of well-built male psych nurses just smirking as I did), I couldn't bullshit my way out of it. I was allowed to call my private GP (at £110 per visit I'd arrogantly assumed he'd be able to sort this) but he simply said there was nothing he could do. I was told to leave my car there and was driven to another hospital about an hour and a half away, crying with rage and frustration.

The intake there was terrifying. I was told to take meds — the first pharmaceutical I'd had in eleven years. When I refused, I was forced to swallow something I couldn't even pronounce. The room spun, my head flew away, everything diminished and I slept for very nearly twenty-four hours flat.

This new hospital was a whole different kettle of mental. It was incredibly meds-friendly. I was basically muzzled with chemicals and left alone for the first few weeks. Getting high after more than a decade drug-free was unpleasant, scary, overwhelming. My short-term memory went immediately — I would introduce myself to the same people again and again — I lost control of my coordination, drooled, sweated all the time. I became a cartoon parody of the 'mental patient'.

Jane and I decided Jack should not come and see me — he shouldn't have to witness me stumbling around, literally walking into walls, unable to focus or speak properly. I became some kind of lab rat for psychiatrists eager to practise their diagnosing and prescribing skills. After a few days I was, apparently, officially suffering from: bipolar disorder, acute PTSD, autism, Tourette's, clinical depression, suicidal ideation, anorexia, DID, borderline personality disorder. And I was medicated 'appropriately'.

Medication is a bastard. I can't tell you. Clonazepam, diazepam, alprazolam, quetiapine, fluoxetine, trimipromine, citalopram, effexor, lithium, tramadol and dozens of others, some at the same time, some cycled through in succession, some combined, some in the evening, some in the morning. And I had no choice — if I refused they were given to me by force.

There was therapy (group and individual) but none of it made any difference at all because I was incapable of lucidity, of rational thought, of any fucking thought at all. They even had me on a drug to help combat self-harm. It was a vicious fucker that stopped the brain releasing endorphins in response to pain, so if I did find a way to cut myself it would just really, really hurt and there would be no high at all. Vile.

Some of the other guys on the ward were genuinely terrifying; one found out I was a pianist and told me he'd break my fingers one by one. Then he just stood really, really still and stared at me, not in a good way. I told him to knock himself out and he still didn't move. So I turned around, closed my eyes and told him I would count to thirty and during that time he could do whatever he wanted to me. He still didn't move. Pussy.

They'd searched me thoroughly and I had nothing to help me die. Everything got too much – guilt at what I was doing to Jack, my fucking head hurt so badly, I couldn't leave, I couldn't stay, I couldn't think, speak, act, dream, imagine. I was stuck in some weird, Big-Pharma-sponsored circle of hell. And there was nothing I could do to escape.

And so I figured I'd tried the 'healthy way' of asking for help. It clearly hadn't worked. And now it was time to do it my way once and for all. Which meant death once again. And planning to kill yourself in a secure ward on a cocktail of mega drugs ain't easy.

I had a mental health nurse (bodyguard) nearby all the time, even when sleeping. There were no blades, sharp objects, no access to the roof, meds were kept ultra-secure under lock and key. So I figured hanging was the only viable option. I knew there was a changeover of my psych guard around 2 a.m. each morning. And I knew that the

TV had a nice long aerial cable. So I pretended I was out cold around 9 p.m. and simply waited. The guy was bored out of his skull and when his replacement arrived they made small talk for a few minutes during the handover. Why wouldn't they? I was dead to the world, it was the middle of the fucking night, the guy was on £8 an hour with better things to think about than keeping an eye on some privileged wanker like me.

They were chatting quietly in the corridor outside my room. I scampered over to the TV set and unplugged the cable. I snuck into the en suite bathroom and stood on the toilet seat, throwing and threading the cable through a vent in the ceiling. I made some kind of noose (not too different from tying a double Windsor), shoved my head through it, gave it a good tug to check it would hold, and jumped.

Thing about hanging – it doesn't strangle you. The whole point is that if you do your calculations correctly, it snaps your neck. Should be over in about 0.6 seconds, lights out, fade to black, done. And had I had the luxury of a giant roof beam, stepladder, proper rope, calculator, internet connection, isolation and Boy-Scout-worthy knot skills it would have been just like that. But no. I fell, nothing snapped (except the last little grubby bit of my mind that was still intact), I saw lots of weird colours, everything become instantly focused and vivid and 'in the moment', and I could feel myself starting to choke. This is the worst thing that can happen with hanging. I couldn't get down to do it again properly; I knew that if I was found I'd be rescued; depending on how long that took I could suffer some kind of brain damage due to oxygen deprivation; and then I'd be (a) forever (more) retarded, and therefore (b) unable to finish the job.

So I'm, quite literally, hanging out in my bathroom and starting to lose consciousness when the door is pushed open and my nurse/bodyguard walks in. His eyes seem to pop out an inch or two, his right hand smacks hard against the wall and bang on top of the panic button, and with the same movement he rushes forward and grabs my legs in a bear hold, lifting me up and shouting for help. I'm not having any of it and start kicking out, wriggling like a motherfucker and grunting, snot pouring out of my nose, spit flying out of my mouth. We're doing this fucked-up kind of salsa dance together when more orderlies run in, assume various positions around me and somehow get me down.

There follows some kind of 'Benny Hill in a psych ward' sketch – I drop into their arms, they relax for a second, I sprint out of the bathroom in my boxer shorts, television aerial around my neck like a pretentious fashion show moment, and start running down the corridors in search of the exit with all the nurses haring after me. Unsurprisingly the ward door is locked, so I grab a giant light stand next to it and start pounding on it. It doesn't budge, I look fucking stupid, and whirl around using the lamp like a *Cuckoo's Nest* light sabre, waving it threateningly at the (ever-growing) group of orderlies fanning out in front of me.

I took seven of them out with my bare hands, threw myself through the door using sheer strength, splintering wood and emerging chrysalis-like into the cold air where I outran the entire security team, boosted over the front barriers and barrelled into a passing cab which screeched off Jack Bauer-style into the night.

Shut up. I lasted about twelve seconds before being pinned to the floor, carried into a secure room, given something awesome to swallow and hurtling down into nothingness.

When I came to, I paid the price. Giant cocktails of drugs, deep and meaningful conversations with the head psychiatrist, room and body searches, no contact with other 'residents' (inmates), meals alone in my room, showers monitored.

You cannot imagine the rage. I didn't know such anger could exist. A constant, cold fury, building up for thirty years and then finally allowed to be unleashed.

I wasn't done yet. Something happened to me. Someone entirely new took charge whose sole mission was to get the fuck out of there. As long as it took, whatever lengths I had to go to. Getting 'well', whatever the fuck that meant, was not going to happen. I could not kill myself in that place and I knew I had to get out of there and find somewhere else to do it.

A few days later I was being taken to see the psychiatrist. There was an office refit going on and he had moved down to the ground floor near the main entrance. Which meant I was escorted (by an even bigger male nurse) out of the locked ward and downstairs. And, remarkably, while I was waiting to see the doc in his sterile but comfortable waiting room, my escort went back up to the ward, leaving me alone. I've no idea why. If it was a communications break-down, laziness, or simply him needing a smoke, but this was my one chance to get out of there and I didn't hesitate. I walked calmly, confidently, to the main doors, pushed them open and walked out into the sunlight. It really was as easy as that. I reckoned I had about a seven-minute head start before anyone clocked what had happened,

I flagged down a cab and asked the guy to take me to Sloane Square tube station.

I paid the driver (I had the princely sum of £70 in cash ostensibly to be used only for buying cigarettes and shit from the hospital 'gift shop'), bought a travel card, jumped into the Tube, went all Jason Bourne by getting on and off trains, taking a bus, changing direction, playing spy for a while, and then ended up in Paddington.

I got razor blades from Boots and wandered around until I'd found the kind of hotel that would make you want to kill yourself even if you were perfectly happy before checking in. It cost me £40, the last of my cash, for the night.

I ran the hottest bath I could bear, laid out my razor blades and towels, undressed and sat on the bed. For the first time in months I could breathe. I was alone, no one knew where I was, I felt quieter than I had in years. I slept for a few hours. Proper, restful sleep, not induced by chemicals, just peaceful, fully clothed, muscles not in spasm, head not in a Magimix.

I knew that I needed to say goodbye to my son. I was fucked, but not so fucked that I could simply exit without him hearing my voice or vice versa. A kind of anchor for him made sense in my mind, so that as he grew up and thought back to when his dad killed himself, he could have some small comfort in knowing he had said goodbye. Such is the narcissism of suicide.

I called his mum's mobile and she answered. Important to note that by now I had basically had a complete break from reality. I wasn't aware of that, but clearly I was functioning on a different operating system from anyone else within a square mile or two. Of course I could call her up, let her know I wanted to speak to my son, had been let out of hospital as a trial to see if I could be trusted to leave for longer periods, and was just checking in. It did not occur to me for a minute that the police may have been contacted, that she had been fielding calls from the hospital and Matthew, all trying to figure out where I was.

And there was still kindness and some kind of love inside her. I don't know why either. But she didn't give me the slightest impression that anything was wrong. She simply said that she would love to see me.

'How about it, Jimmy? I could come meet you anywhere – we could have a quick ten minutes together and then you can either come home for a bit or not. Up to you.'

And I figured, with the kind of fucked-up, egocentric nobility that can only come from a psychotic break and the heinous amount of meds still in my system, that yes, this was an excellent idea. I shall see my wife for a proper goodbye, kiss her one final time and then come back here and do what needs to be done. Because that is the right thing to do. The right thing to do.

I left everything as it was, laid out OCD-style on the bed, evenly spaced, correctly angled, checked and double-checked, and wandered out of the room towards Paddington station where we'd arranged to meet on the main concourse.

I got there and stood watching the harried, drunk, lost and busy commuters rushing around for twenty minutes until I saw Jane. And Jack. For some unimaginable reason she had brought him with her. A real-life, 3-foot-tall surprise on her part, albeit with the best of intentions. He was tiny. A little bundle of Puffa jacket and impossibly small denim jeans, holding her hand. As I walked down the escalator towards them I could feel something in my heart thudding and pounding and cracking. And on I walked until he saw me and ran towards me. That hug was every bit as memorable and important as the one I gave him when he was first handed to me in the hospital moments after he was born. And before we even had a chance to say anything, I knew something deep down had shifted.

Out of the corner of my eye I saw Matthew coming towards me. He had spoken with the police, I was going to be back in hospital within half an hour. And I wasn't even angry. Relieved, perhaps, more than anything. Because there was a new feeling way down at the bottom of things, trying to get heard. Something happened when Jack's tiny, sweaty hand grasped mine and squeezed it harder than I'd thought possible. When I smelled his little head and felt him barrelling into me shouting 'Daddy', it was a primal, lizard-brain biological imperative along the lines of 'Well, you've abandoned yourself, but it goes against the fundamental nature of things to do the same to him, and you know it.' He was an extension of me. A part of me. If the host died then the rest of the organism would also die, and he wasn't strong enough to exist without me at that point.

I wasn't ready to go yet. And if I hadn't called Jane, if she hadn't played me, if I hadn't seen Jack one last time, I would never have heard that inner shout loudly enough to pay attention to it.

I was driven back to hospital.

It felt like all the fight had been kicked out of me. I was floppy, pliable, indifferent. Shuffling around the ward, dribbling a bit, losing a few more brain cells and memories thanks to yet another cocktail of meds. And then on a visitors' Sunday I was called in and told someone was there to see me. Which was odd because aside from a brief, disastrous visit from Jane and Jack a few weeks previously, I'd never had a visitor before.

It was an old pal I hadn't seen in a long time. An awkward, slightly autistic, fragile guy. A piano fanatic (we'd met because we'd both shared a mutual hard-on for Sokolov bootlegs back in the day). He'd heard I was there and wanted to offer support. And music. When he'd called to arrange the visit he'd been told that no presents other than toiletries etc were permitted (I wasn't allowed to have things delivered to me by this stage because I'd already had knives and razors intercepted). He offered me a giant bottle of shampoo and winked at me. Out of earshot of the nurses he told me to open it up when I was alone. Which I did. And inside this emptied bottle was a tiny plastic bag. And inside the tiny plastic bag was the brand new, recently launched iPod nano. It was the size of an After Eight mint. And the headphones were wrapped around it lovingly. He had filled it up with gigabytes of music. And everything changed.

Under the covers I went. Headphones on. Middle of the night. Dark and impossibly quiet. And I hit play and heard a piece by Bach that I'd not heard before. And it took me to a place of such magnificence, such surrender, hope, beauty, infinite space, it was like touching God's face. I swear I had some kind of spiritual epiphany then and there. The piece was the Bach-Marcello Adagio – a work written for oboe and orchestra by a baroque composer called Alessandro Marcello that Bach loved so much he transcribed it for solo piano. Glenn Gould was playing his Steinway, reaching out from forty years in the past, three hundred years in the past, and letting me know that things were not only going to be OK, they were going to be absolutely fucking stellar. It felt like I'd been plugged into an electrical socket. It was one of those rare 'Elvis moments' that I will never forget. It shattered me and released some kind of inner gentleness that hadn't seen the light of day for thirty years.

And now I was determined. I knew this place wasn't the right place for me. I could not get well. Not with so many meds, so much madness, so much daytime TV and boredom. I needed to get out of there properly, once and for all. Get released, find some space, get home to my son. I needed to get well. But first I needed to show them I was well enough to leave.

And so I did. We did. That cold, ruthless, patient, clever fucker who controlled some part of my mind took charge. Happily. He was born for this shit. We started cooperating, not too quickly to make it unrealistic, nor too slowly to miss my self-imposed deadline of a Christmas release. I cried on demand, hugged my inner child, drew appropriately angry pictures in art therapy, participated in group sessions, came across with just the right amount of concern, remorse, anger, hope, contrition in my individual therapy. I sat through hearings and interviews saying the right things and then backed that up with doing the right actions. I helped others, cracked jokes with the staff, started whistling happily within earshot of the doctors, took my meds, got up early and meditated in the garden in full view of the night staff. I did everything I needed to in order to get to that Monday afternoon two months later in mid-November when they sat me down, basically told me I was a poster boy for mental health treatment, they were delighted with my progress and were very pleased to tell me I had been given the all-clear. I could leave in three days, as long as I agreed to a vigorous outpatient follow-up course and maintained my medication routine.

My grateful, solicitous, faux-humble smile was Oscar-worthy. I even included the obligatory 'Are you sure I'm ready for this?' routine, voicing my concerns. I got them to actually convince me to leave. Mark Rylance would have applauded my performance. I was stupidly proud of what I'd accomplished, and three days later strutted out of that hospital, ditched my meds and went home to bed.

A quick aside about the rather nonchalant 'ditched my meds' bit. Do not, under any circumstances, do that. Not ever. Imagine squeezing a giant dollop of properly homemade mayonnaise onto a piece of raw chicken, leaving it out in the sun for four or five days and then shoving the whole thing into your mouth, lying down in bed and waiting. And you will come close to what it's like to come off psychotropic medication cold turkey.

It took around twelve hours before the brain shakes started to come. Everything began to feel very surreal, slightly drunken, not quite concrete. Over time that turned into hallucinations, muscle spasms, puking, shitting, heaving, sweating, aching, shaking, retching. I was out of commission for three days before feeling vaguely able to walk, talk, function.

I'd had such high hopes that I would get out of hospital, return to a home filled with love and support and that all would be well. That the lightning bolt of hope that my illicit music stash had brought me in hospital would persist and flourish on the outside. But of course that didn't happen. I was a fucking liability, there were bills to pay, paperwork to organise, shit to deal with. My piano had to be sold for a fraction of what we had paid for it so my one potential lifeline was out of the window. Things felt tense, hostile, scary, uneasy and uncertain at home. We were all in the hole with no idea how to get out of it or whether that was even possible. Things had gone so wrong, so quickly, it felt like there was no way back.

Just because I had slowed my life down didn't mean the real world had slowed down for one minute. It had been zipping along while I was totally oblivious and I was trying to play catch-up without any of the skills necessary to do so. It was the first time I truly realised that good intentions were no longer enough. Even out of hospital, off meds, physically present for my family, I was a ghost.

Despite wanting one, I didn't feel a connection to my wife any more, no optimistic future binding us together or hopes and dreams to talk about late into the night. I had sleepwalked into this relationship, had a perfect, beautiful and amazing child and no idea how to bring him up. They say marriage is hard work. I had no idea just what that meant until I looked around and realised I had absented myself from it both emotionally and physically for the better part of a year, was floundering about like a sick fish out of water and now, having been kept alive in hospital but not given the skills necessary to do the same for my marriage, I needed to find a way to repair untold damage.

And then a friend of ours offered me a lifeline. A one-shot deal that could possibly mend things.

This guy was rich. Stupidly rich. Homes around the world,

private-jets-and-submarines rich. He knew us well, had been in close contact with my wife, seen what was happening. He'd had his own demons to battle back in the day and had gone to some place in Arizona that had helped him. He saw that I wasn't getting well, whatever that meant, that I hadn't even begun to deal with the stuff that had put me in hospital to begin with, that I was still a ticking bomb. And he offered to pay for me to go to that place he had gone to.

He gave them a lot of money every year, which was lucky because he had called them and they had unanimously voted to not accept me. They had read the medical notes and felt I was much too high a risk for them. But Bob, my rich friend, made it clear they would not get another cent out of him unless they admitted me for as long as it took. And money trumps everything in the psychiatric profession.

Bob called me up. He said to me that without this place in Phoenix he wouldn't be here, that no matter how much I wanted to be well and happy and healthy, unless I did the work it just wasn't going to happen, and that going to this hospital for a few weeks would be a springboard back into life for both me and my marriage. He said I was unwell, and that without help it was only going to get worse. I'd spent the previous afternoon holding an ice pack to my groin for an hour, attempting to summon up the courage to castrate myself, so he had no argument from me.

And so, once again, I packed my bag, left my family and boarded a plane to indulge in a little US-style therapy in Phoenix.

Mozart, Symphony No. 41 ('Jupiter'), Fourth Movement
Sir Charles Mackerras, Conductor

The world's most famous composer. It's quite an achievement and yet somehow one feels Mozart wouldn't have given two fucks. Bringing a whole new definition to the word 'genius' (composing from the age of five, touring from six, able to speak fifteen languages, writing forty-one symphonies, twenty-seven piano concertos, numerous operas, chamber music and sonatas etc etc), the depth of Mozart's monumental talent was only matched by the length of his name, Johannes Theophilus Amadeus Gottlieb Chrysostomus Wolfgangus Sigismundus Mozart.

Three years before he died at the age of thirty-five, Mozart composed his greatest and last symphony – his forty-first (it was christened the 'Jupiter' twenty-six years after his death in a piece of marketing spin that had nothing to do with Mozart himself). He composed it in sixteen days and it represents the sum total of his mastery of composition. At the same time he wrote both his thirty-ninth and fortieth symphonies; three enduring masterpieces written within days of one another and in such a short period of time gives us an idea of the outrageousness of Mozart's skills.

Right at the end of the last movement of the forty-first he opens the final coda with a five-part fugue — an astonishing, miraculous piece of orchestral writing that has never been bettered. Imagine the same theme being played five times over but with each one entering after a delayed start, and all of them need to combine together to make perfect harmonic sense with a hundred musicians playing at full pelt. He waits until the last forty-five seconds of the whole symphony before doing it (because it's the musical equivalent of juggling fifteen chainsaws and any longer is just about impossible) and it's the reason I could never play an orchestral instrument — I would literally piss myself with joy and collapse if I were ever to play that on stage.

There are two quotes that are apposite here, the first by Schumann, who said of the 'Jupiter': 'There are things in the world about which nothing can be said, as Mozart's "Jupiter" Symphony with the fugue, much of Shakespeare, and pages of Beethoven.'

And regarding that bloody fugue, which is still just about the most exciting thing I've ever heard an orchestra play, Sir Donald Francis Tovey wrote:

'Each movement of the "Jupiter" symphony is a powerful and surpassing creation. The capstone of this towering symphony is of course the fugue-finale, wherein the polyphonic workmanship of the old fugue is used, with other material, for the perfect consummation of the composer's thought, and the eternal glory of art. There is indeed no match for this movement in the literature of the symphony. There are other compositions — a few equal to it in interest — but

there are no others like it, even in Mozart. That is his symphonic apotheosis
— the fugue-finale of the "Jupiter" symphony.'

AMERICA'S ALWAYS A BIT BIGGER, brasher, more in your face than anywhere else. The same is true of their mental health industry. Having successfully navigated their landing card (I don't have affiliations with the Nazi party and haven't yet participated in genocide or nuclear weapons manufacturing, but the drug addiction and mental illness questions were treated with some poetic licence). I was met at Phoenix's Sky Harbor airport by two stupidly big dudes in Stetsons and driven to what looked like a prison. Security guards with Tasers, truncheons and mace patrolling around, obligatory Ray-Bans and failed-cop-attitude as much a part of their uniform as their lack of compassion and steroid-induced biceps. Which was like a red rag to a bull for me. I was instantly aggressive, full of piss and vinegar, provocative, obtuse, violent. Bizarrely, I felt these guys could handle my misdirected anger, being armed and all, and I just let go. It all came out. I gave them everything I had and then some.

Intake, in fact the whole admissions process, was harsh — it was like boot camp for nutjobs. I made it harsher. Everything was taken. And I mean everything. Books, music, phones, cash, keys, passport — all removed. Strip-searches, blood tests, urine tests, psychometric evaluations, endless questionnaires, interviews, interrogations. I was given new meds (no idea which) and told that before I would be allowed to join the rest of the patients I would spend the usual three days in a room by the nurses' station, with a bodyguard for my own protection within arm's reach of me at all times. This was standard procedure that everyone underwent upon admission. Only it wasn't the usual three days. I spent seventeen days in that room (a record, they've since told me), howling, yelling, raging, trying to fuck myself up in every way I could. It got so bad (certain things, certain levels of violence and dysfunction I cannot bring myself to write about here) that after a couple of weeks of this they were willing to say goodbye to Bob's yearly donations and involve the police. I was to be picked up, arrested, and taken to a federal psychiatric institution where there was 'an outside chance you'll make it out within a year or two'.

Handy hint – should you ever want someone like me (a petulant, lost, frightened, psychopathic egomaniac) to cooperate fully and immediately, simply mention the words 'federal' and 'institution' and bring a straitjacket into the room and lay it out on the bed. I have never snapped out of something so quickly.

I genuinely hit my knees and begged them not to take me. I talked as fast and as honestly as I could in between sobs, and finally was granted a twenty-four-hour reprieve. One last chance. A one-shot deal. Any hint of being a dickhead and I would be lost in the system, away from anyone and everyone I knew and out of commission for a long time. They could do that with one phone call.

A couple of days later they could see they'd got through to me. Whatever resistance I'd had left had been ripped out of me and I was allowed to join the others. The weirdest, most motley crew of individuals imaginable, and all of them were completely lovely. Some were wearing stickers saying 'men only' (raging sex addicts who were not allowed to speak to any women, ever); some were stupidly young (seventeen-year-old boys and girls who were part of the OxyContin epidemic); some were decent, handsome, wealthy businessmen and women; some were broke, homeless guys off the street; all were kind, all seemed to be open to the idea that they could get well.

And so it began. I listened for a few days without joining in or speaking in any of the group meetings or therapy sessions. I watched and waited and looked for the trap, the con, the reason why this wouldn't work for me. I had had no hope for so long I just couldn't see things differently. But ever so slowly, something began to lift and there was a creeping sense of safety emerging each day.

And that is where things finally, miraculously, began to turn around.

I don't know if it was osmosis, or simply tiredness. Perhaps it was that they had weaned me off all medication except at night time. But, with honest and decent motives, I began to open up a little bit, participate in therapy, talk to other patients and staff. And the staff were brilliant there – well trained, empathic, kind, insightful. There was a lot of work to be done, a lot of writing, reading, exploring, digging, discovering and talking. There was meditation every day, group therapy, one-on-one therapy, new US-centric therapies with awesome names such as 'somatic experiencing' and 'survivors' workshops'. I hit things with giant plastic batons, talked about what had happened when I was a kid, and saw that it was met with horror and compassion rather than disbelief and blame. I cried, wrote hypothetical letters to the gym teacher, Mr Lee, found some way to let myself off the hook for being so promiscuous and slutty when I was a pre-teen boy, began to understand how the wiring in my brain had been broken and re-soldered at a young age, how I'd been in survival mode for decades, how although I was responsible for my life, I was not to blame for it.

Giant things started to happen inside me. Huge shifts in thinking and reasoning began to take shape. These guys really got me. They met my crazy with total understanding and acceptance, and they offered me solutions to problems that had seemed insurmountable. We spent weeks going back over my life, looking at my part in everything. Seeing where I had been responsible for things – where I had been selfish, self-centred, dishonest, self-seeking, manipulative, scared. Why I had acted the way I had, who I had hurt and how. I wrote every-thing down and made a list of everyone whose life I had impacted on negatively. It was a long one. Then we figured out all of those people to whom I owed some kind of apology or amends. Again, a long one.

There were institutions like schools and universities and workplaces I'd stolen from (stolen not just tangible things like money, but also time); places and people I'd gossiped about (apparently this is not OK, no matter how trivial it had seemed to me at the time); property I'd destroyed or vandalised; friends I'd ignored or damaged; relationships where I'd been self-centred or manipulative (everyone I'd slept with, basically); my family whom I'd caused to worry, whose lives I'd disrupted, whose peace of mind I'd stolen; friends, colleagues, acquaint-ances whom I'd hurt. Anyone at all who, were I to see them walking towards me would make me want to cross the street to avoid them, went on the list. The rule of thumb was that unless making amends to these people would cause them further distress ('I slept with your girlfriend/wife/daughter, sorry about that') they needed to be approached and action taken.

The hospital gave me a phone and a computer and I wrote to or called every one of the people on my list apologising, owning up to my part in things, asking if there was anything I could do to make amends. Most of the people involved were simply pleased, if slightly bemused, to hear from me. Some of them didn't want to talk. A few of them were really happy to get things off their chest. This was not about inviting punishment or blame or recrimination. It was about making sure I could sleep well at night. About knowing that I could have contact, intentional or accidental, with anybody from my past without my stomach being gripped by shame and fear. And so, where appropriate, I apologised, donated money, paid back money, offered to do anything and everything I could to make things right.

There was a slightly Bible-Belt slant towards religion in the work we did there, but they dressed it up believably as spirituality and I figured who the fuck was I to deny the existence of something bigger than me that somehow made things function. It was a bit of a relief to allow myself to resign as general manager of the whole fucking universe and simply wander around as a part of it for once. I think they call it 'humility'.

I was there for two months in total. By the end of it I had, miraculously, stopped hating myself quite so much. I'd put on weight, cleared away a lot of the wreckage of the past, repaired some relationships and found a way to live with myself that, most days, left me relatively calm and composed.

I'd been speaking with Jack a couple of times a week and was hungry to see him. I was finally able to show up now. And maybe that would be enough to rebuild things between me and Jane and create a proper little family unit the way we'd both wanted to way back when.

It was a feeling of surrender. I'd somehow got enough clarity and self-awareness to know that I was able now to do all I could to get well, that I had the tools necessary to slowly move forward without destroying shit. And I also knew that there was no guarantee that those around me would believe that. I was going home to an unknown entity.

It was terrifying and exciting all at once. Time maybe to have a cup of tea and have a listen to Chopin's greatest nocturne – the one in C minor Op. 48/1 (YouTube, Spotify, iTunes, SoundCloud, take your pick). That's what it felt like: full of trepidation, longing, stormy emotions, uncertainty, restlessness, surrender and hope. All the things I imagine Chopin himself must have felt when, as a twenty-year-old, he left his home in Warsaw to go and explore the world.

He ended up in Paris because he couldn't get into Austria (his first choice), caught a dose of something from a hooker, was violently homesick, a bit of an asshole, uncertain and unsure. He wrote his first piano concerto aged nineteen, and in the following twenty years he changed the world of the piano forever.

He was, of course, also royally fucked by his incredibly dysfunctional relationship with George Sand, broke, sick, miserable, and died, in agony, of consumption at the age of thirty-nine.

Me, I was slightly less broke, monumentally less talented, perhaps just as sick, not quite as miserable and not yet coughing up bits of my lungs.

I said my goodbyes, thanked the staff, packed my bag, and flew back to London. No bodyguards this time. No meds. No hidden razor blades. It felt like a new beginning, and it turned out that's exactly what it was, just not in the way I had imagined. Not in the way anyone could have predicted.

I walked through my front door to my wife and son. They'd put up 'welcome home' signs and made cakes. I felt like I was properly back home then. I knew I'd be a better dad to Jack from that moment. That I would be present and available and strong. I knew I would have to prove that to him over time. That after so many months of being away with only occasional contact it would take a while for him to learn he could rely on me again. Five-year-olds are sentient enough. I had to earn his trust again and I was fully prepared to go to any lengths to do that.

And so I did. I spent as much time as I could with him. And the truth was that we had spent so much time together during his first three or four years on this Earth, I had spent so many nights and days feeding him, walking him, soothing him, we had had such a deep bond back then, that it wasn't long until it started to come back. That's the weird thing about kids – they have a capacity for forgiveness that most adults can only aspire to. He had always loved me – it was inbuilt and immutable – and I him. After a few weeks of playing, singing, hanging out, we felt absolutely connected and back to normal. I dropped him off and picked him up from school each day, took him to the park, built Lego and took him to Starbucks for treats, read to him, watched TV with him, fed him, hugged him, generally let him know I was there.

I felt like the biggest amends I had to make were to him, and the only way of doing that was by showing him he could count on me. And stupidly, perhaps naively, I didn't do the same with Jane. All my attention was on Jack, and things between his mother and me were slipping away a little more each day.

There are a few things I know about love today that seem to have only become apparent after thirty years of total stupidity and a few shorter years of intense self-searching and examination. Unfortunately love is always a practical exam, never theoretical, and all the thinking in the world is ultimately pointless. It's like learning to play the piano by reading a manual. You might think you know what to do, but until you're sat at the keyboard and discover how immensely, overwhelmingly complex it is, how much effort and concentration is required, you know nothing.

I hate the expression 'falling in love'. It's bollocks. You don't fall anywhere. Falling in love implies you shoot down the mine shaft and end up alone and smashed up at the bottom, half dead. Everything today has got so immediate, so big, so much harder and faster and wilder and shinier than it used to be. *Inspector Morse* used to seem fast-paced and edge-of-your-seat. Nowadays no one in their right minds would dare to commission a mainstream TV show with titles lasting longer than seven seconds. So today, 'falling in love' doesn't mean courting, dating and spending weeks getting to know one another, going on a journey together and over time realising you are both deeply in love. It means it's exactly as it is in the movies – your eyes meet (or you see her Twitter avatar), you exchange a word, text, email or two and then BANG, you're in love. Urgent, immediate, explosive, hot. You tell all your friends, post it all over Facebook and act like a giant fuck-nugget. It's Disney on crack and it's fucking dangerous. Nothing can be sustained like that. There can never be any truth in it. It is simply addiction, brain chemicals getting you higher and higher before the inevitable crash. But we all play along because that's how it works in movies and on TV and in the papers and it's alluring and immediate and frisky.

My marriage was, in effect, a dress rehearsal for the real thing. And it came at an astonishing price. Despite not having a proper foundation from the get-go and being emotionally retarded when Jane and I first met, I thought I'd fallen in love. But in hindsight perhaps I'd just fallen. Fallen into the fantasy of love, ignoring the reality, buying into the whole bullshit make-believe of romance and adventure. Today I much prefer the idea of walking beside one another in love, rather than falling. Of keeping my eyes wide open, not masked by cynicism or closed by fear, but looking for and offering qualities that I'd never deemed terribly important before now. Kindness, compassion, depth, patience and so on.

I know I can be happy for the rest of my life with the woman I am with now. I know it on a cellular level. I also know that men always want to leave. We are conditioned to. And so we will always question things, usually to ourselves, occasionally to our friends, rarely, and stupidly, to our lovers. That little voice will always believe there is someone cuter, less needy, dirtier in bed, more independent, nicer-smelling, cooler, whatever the fuck. Just like the new iPhone feels redundant after three months. The TV after five years. The suit, job, car, house. Everything needs to be better all the time, and if we realise that our wife isn't going to defy the laws of biology and physics and get prettier, more streamlined, faster, newer, upgraded we freak out.

And then we have affairs, start drinking, pick fights. There was no cheating or drinking, but my behaviour around Jane became more destructive and more critical over time. It became, in my head at least, a near constant state of conflict, arguments happening not just at times of stress but at the drop of a hat. Needling, whining, judging. And then, finally, the killer blow – indifference. The vile apathy of 'Who gives a fuck?' And even when it gets to that advanced stage of shit in a relationship, most of us men are too much of a pussy to up and leave and so we try and get our women to do it for us. We become intolerable in the hope that they will file for divorce and we can go on to do the same thing with the next woman. No wonder couples therapy is such a fast-growing business.

Jane and I agreed to a trial separation and I moved out.

It didn't matter that separating was the right course of action. That, long-term, it was most definitely for the best. I'd become one of those men. Quitters. The ones who bail when it gets too fucking real. I rented a little basement flat, got a shitty upright piano in there, made sure I had a spare room for Jack to sleep in, woke up early every morning to collect him and take him to school on the bus (we'd sold the car by now). I did all I could to be the best dad I could be for him. But I was still a quitter. I could fast-forward in my head to a few years down the line when my therapised son says to me, 'Dad, you abandoned me', and find nothing to counter that.

Things started to get more and more wobbly. It wasn't helped by my going to the police to try and exorcise some of the past horrors.

They have a child protection unit in Earl's Court. I went to make a statement about Mr Lee and see if they could track him down and make him accountable. I did it for closure, for justice, to try and make amends to the little me and to continue the healthy start I had made in Phoenix. It was hopeless. And excruciating. I spent about three hours in front of a video camera giving details no one should have to give. Diagrams of the gym, what happened where, how often, where he came, when, what kind of sex, what positions, what implements he used, did I swallow, what did it taste like (seriously) and on and on. It was brutal, shaming, vile. And after all that they told me that they had got in touch with the school and that they had no record of someone of that name ever working there. The police assumed it was a false name, they couldn't find him and nothing could be done.

Any progress I had made from my stay at Phoenix seemed to vanish at this point. I bought blades again and started to cut. I stopped eating. By this time, Bob seemed to have had enough of my descent into victimhood. He asked me to pay him back every penny he had spent on the hospital in Phoenix (a bowel-loosening amount that decimated my bank account and gave me another reason to feel sick with worry and self-hatred). I did anything I could do to punish myself. Which, again, is lovely in a selfish way as the pay-off and feelings of self-hatred are glorious, but the knock-on effect is often disastrous.

One ray of sunshine: I had a new psychiatrist called Billy. A tall, softly spoken, kind and easy-going Irishman. The first time I saw him, shortly after returning to London from hospital, he said to me, in his awesome Cork-drenched voice, 'Ah James, honestly it's fifty-fifty if you'll be here in a year. I know that and you know that. Some people make it and others, well they don't get to come out the other side. That's the way it is. Let's see what we can do to boost your chances a bit, eh?' And right then I knew he was perfect. To acknowledge what I'd always known and what no one had ever voiced before, to do it so matter-of-factly and calmly, and to not go down the whole 'inspire through psychobabble' bullshit routine was so refreshing I almost applauded. He's done more than I could ever have hoped to keep me well (he still does), but it was, is, a long process. And back then the allure of the razor blade was still so fucking strong.

This relapse into cutting meant that I was no longer allowed to see Jack unsupervised. My rage and frustration at the total breakdown in communication between Jane and me grew and grew and there was nothing I could do about it. There is this one thing. This single 'trigger' that makes me angrier than anything else. It is when I feel someone is ignoring me, not hearing me, not seeing me. The irony that I do the same thing all the time by zoning out when I'm around people doesn't escape me. I can ask someone a question and if they ignore me I automatically react inside my head with thirty years of rage. I ask a girlfriend, 'Hey, shall we go shopping tomorrow?' – she's reading something, doesn't hear me so doesn't respond, and I feel like she's literally just fucked her yoga teacher in front of me while laughing and joking about what a puny turd I am and I just want to die. I'm well aware that this is a recurring, paranoid theme of mine. No doubt it comes from begging the teacher to stop fucking me and him doing the opposite. Or perhaps from begging other teachers or my parents not to send me to gym class and being ignored. Either way, it's my thing. We all have one, right?

I kept trying to explain to Jane what was going on, that I wasn't a threat, that we could work things out, that there was no need to enforce supervised access to Jack, but I felt I got nowhere. The irritation and sense of being unheard grew and grew, I could see my son slowly being taken away from me, no one willing to listen to me or understand what was going on in my head. Until I lost it.

And I was off. Right back at square one. Terrified, hurtling down the hole. Convinced I was going to be sectioned. I could not, would not, allow that to happen. I jumped in a cab with my passport and told the cabbie to take me to Heathrow. On the way I booked the first international flight I could find (to New York, as it happened), arrived at Terminal 3, withdrew pretty much my last $5,000 in cash, boarded the plane and fled the country. I had no idea why, what I was going to do, if I would simply spend the cash on hookers and drink and coke and then shoot myself in the head. I just had to run. Somehow all of this seemed easier and made more sense than just sitting calmly with the doctors and trying to find a solution that worked for all of us. Yep. Off I went again, not telling anyone where I was going, no idea for how long, leaving my wife and son alone.

I was away for a week. During that time I spent hours at a kick-boxing gym in Manhattan getting the shit kicked out of me by a 4-foot-wide Puerto Rican black belt (excellent punishment), trying to think straight and sort out what was happening. I emailed my wife and then spoke to her on the phone. I apologised. Tried to explain what was happening in my head and that I didn't want it to be like this any more. She told me she wanted a divorce. I asked her to think about it for a while, that something like this was a huge decision, and would she at least take a few weeks to consider it. And if she still wanted to go through with it I said I wouldn't contest anything. There was no need for lawyers – we could do one of those quickie online things if that was what she really wanted and she could have anything she wanted from me as long as I could have access to Jack.

Very soon after I got home from New York there were papers waiting for me from her lawyer. I'd finally pushed her to breaking point.

And I started to unravel again like some broken fucking record. I lost so much weight my doctor told me that within three months my lungs and brain would begin to shut down and that if I didn't start to consume at least eight hundred calories a day he would section me. I was cutting regularly, sleeping around two to three hours a night, trying so hard to find something about myself that wasn't toxic and broken.

I had to get my own divorce lawyer but I still didn't care and just told the guy I'd happily sign whatever. More punishment, more desperate attempts to absolve myself of the guilt of exploding my family.

And just like that, I was on my own. There was something incredibly freeing about having a small, finite amount of money in the bank, a 350-square-foot basement flat rented and paid in advance for 6 months, and no career. I can't explain it. Almost all of the cash I'd been left with, post separation and divorce, had been spent on paying Bob back, rent and my escape to New York, and things suddenly got very simple. Easier to handle. I'd pick Jack up from school on the

Friday and we'd hang out until I dropped him home the next day. Communications with Jane were not good. It was like a switch being flipped. We had become two separate, coldly civil strangers. My only concern was Jack, my shame, remorse and guilt overwhelming.

Chopin Étude in C major, Op. 10/1
Maurizio Pollini, Piano

Chopin. There are so many self-imposed rules about concerts today, perhaps I could add one of my own?

Every piano recital should include at least one piece by Chopin.

He was a music freak from some tiny village outside Warsaw who revolutionised piano playing forever. The only composer I can think of, perhaps with the exception of Ravel, about whom one can say that 99 per cent of everything he ever wrote is still in active repertory today.

He wrote almost exclusively for the piano, and despite being rather unlikeable (a social climber, slightly racist, financially reckless) changed the musical landscape so completely and so dramatically that it is simply not possible to talk about piano music without mentioning him. He experimented with and created a new piano sonority that once and for all released the instrument from the past. It's no wonder he could charge the equivalent of £900 an hour for piano lessons.

One of the first cassettes I bought was of the great Italian pianist Maurizio Pollini playing Chopin's études. These bastard difficult pieces were designed, as are all studies, to improve technical proficiency. But unlike what had come before him (dull, interminable exercises with little or no musical content via composers like Hanon and Czerny), each of the twenty-seven he wrote is a genuine miniature masterpiece of melody, form, beauty and technical pyrotechnics.

And he doesn't make you hang around waiting for the good stuff until the third or fourth étude either; straight out of the gate he opens with the hardest of them all, a visceral display of giant, near-impossible-to-stretch arpeggios flying up and down the keyboard like a hand possessed.

There is a perception of Chopin as an effete, slight, fragile man-child, incapable of strength and force. These pieces, like so many others, blow that preconception out of the water.

I KNEW JACK WOULD NEED me more than ever now, even if the time we spent together was only a couple of days a week, and I needed to get in shape for him, even if I couldn't do it for me. Having moved out of our home, and with little else to do, I started getting more and more involved in the piano again. I had to, or else I'd sink without trace. I started learning new pieces, practising, listening, working properly. Over a few weeks, with the help of a decent shrink, some space, good food, Matthew and a couple of new close friends, my head became if not quieter, then at least more manageable. Some of the old feelings from America came back – good feelings of hope and potential and freedom. I stopped cutting, started eating, was present with my son when I was around him (the opposite of so many fathers I see glued to their smartphones whilst apparently spending quality time with their kids). And, as if some weird karmic debt were finally being repaid in tiny instalments, something wonderful happened. I was broke, alone, uncertain about every area of my life, and one day, in a café, I walked straight into the man who would become my manager and change my life forever.

I like talking to strangers. I read a book about depression once where the protagonist was so lonely she used to join queues simply for the human interaction. And while things weren't quite that bad yet, I did at times strike up conversations with people. Never on the Tube, of course; certain things are absolute no-nos. But cafés were fair game, and in the queue one morning I got talking to a Canadian guy. He was maybe fifteen years older than me, had a sweet hockey body, a bit of a beard and a kind face. Turns out he was a restaurateur who'd sold his business for a pretty decent wedge and was kicking around London, his spiritual home of many years, looking for a new project. And boy did he find one.

His name was Denis. And that's 'Denis', rhyming with Lenny but with the stress on the last syllable. It's French Canadian. It is not Dennis (as in menace). Nor is it Denny (as in Crane, of Crane, Poole & Schmidt). He has asked me specifically to point that out. Which I've just done. But do feel free to call him Dennis should you meet him, just to see him wince.

Thing is, this had to be a genuine cosmic coincidence. Denis knew almost nothing about classical music. And of course when he asked me what I did, and I told him I was trying to become a concert pianist, there was that slightly awkward silence where neither of us knew what to say. And then he says to me:

'I only really know one piece of piano music. A friend of mine was obsessed with it and he used to play it to me all the time. It's called the Bach-Busoni Chaconne. Do you know it?'

I shit you not. The one piece of music which I had carried around in my heart since the age of seven, that had got me through rocky, desperate, brutal years, and that I had recently brought back to a vaguely decent standard on my little piano in my tiny flat. It felt like the universe saying, 'Hey man – see what happens now you've stopped being a giant dick!'

So of course I squeal like a stuck pig and do a little dance, hopping from foot to foot. And once I realise he hasn't backed out of the door slowly, I let him know that it's my favourite piece ever.

'I should play it to you let's go down to Steinway fuck I can't believe you know that piece dude it's so awesome have you heard Kissin play it oh man they say Russians can't really do Bach but it's the shit I swear you know it was originally for violin but boy does it sound better on a piano doesn't everything I bet if Bach had a modern piano he'd have done it himself have you heard Michelangeli play it oh my GOD . . .' etc etc.

Shut up. I was excited.

Turns out he's killing some time and we wander down to Marylebone Lane with me rattling on at fifty miles an hour about the piece, about Bach losing pretty much everyone he loved and most of his kids, about the fact that he missed like 40 per cent of his schooling because of the violence going on both there and at home, and what a fucking legend he was and that this piece was some kind of musical homage to his dead wife, and imagine that, putting into music something that words cannot express and taking us on this journey of grief until the very end when he leaves it up to us the performer to decide if we want to finish on a major chord (yay!) or a minor chord (shoot me now) and on and on and on until we're right there in the Steinway showroom by one of their 9-foot grand pianos and he sits down and I sit down and I mumble about it being fifteen minutes long and hope that's OK and that I haven't warmed up and so on and then I start playing and what feels like fourteen seconds later I bounce up having finished and say 'Let's go get some coffee! I'm dying for a smoke. Jesus what a piece, huh? Did you hear all those hidden inner voices? Wonder if they were real voices to him' (another etc etc, sorry) and we wander (he wanders, I bounce Tigger-like) down the road to another franchised excuse for a café.

And finally when I pause for breath he's all emotional and shook up and a bit teary and tells me it was beyond amazing, that he had no idea about the stuff I was talking about but it added so much to the piece knowing its history, and where could he buy my albums. And I started laughing because of the whole album thing and the fact that me having an album was as likely as me fucking Alexa Chung. And he says, 'Well why not put some figures on paper and bring it to me and maybe I can help you make one?'

And everything changed. Kapow.

So I call a guy who calls a guy who knows a guy who calls a guy and I find a guy who can produce an album. He helps me find a sound guy and a studio. I get some rough prices, scribble them down on an envelope and rush round to Denis' flat. I tell him *nothing* about my history other than vaguely hinting I'd had a tricky time a while ago, we agree terms and percentages and stuff that means absolutely nothing to me because I'm going to record an album and that's literally all I can think about, and he draws up a contract and I sign it and then fuck me if two weeks later I'm driving with him down to Suffolk to record my very own CD.

We talk a bit in the car and I tell him about hospital and my head and whatnot. And that I only got out very recently and even though I may have given him the impression I'd had some emotional trouble 'a few years ago', I hadn't been entirely honest about timescales and severity, but all was OK now, I promise, no worries, let's go make a record, I don't need more meds, I swear it.

And he says, 'Do you mind if we pull over so I can have a piss?'

So we do, and I have a long moment where I think, Jesus Christ that's it, I'm never going to see him again because I'm mental and now he knows I've only been out of hospital a few weeks and of course no one in their right minds would take on someone like me, let alone lay out a huge chunk of cash for the privilege, and right now he's haring back to London as fast as he can while I'm waiting here like a muppet, all excited about making an album.

And then he climbs back in, and somehow, miraculously, we drive on. And maybe out of the corner of my eye I catch a wry grin pass over his kind face.

Glenn Gould, my hero, talked about the sanctity of the recording studio, the 'womb-like security' of it. And yes. Me in a giant room. In a barn in a field. Alone. With a jumbo, mega piano. No cars, trains, planes. Plenty of coffee. Kit Kats. Music scores. Cigarettes.

Next door in the control room: sound guy, engineer, producer, manager.

Four days allocated when I know I only need two, but he's paying and I need extra time to satisfy my crazy.

So we start with Bach. Of course. His Fifth French Suite. And I start to play it through. And the producer starts telling the guys in the booth how weird it sounds, how slow, or romantic or odd. And then he slows down. Then he stops talking completely. And twenty minutes later he's all pleased and excited and happy and moved and shit. And on we go. Chopin, Beethoven, Moszkowski, and then the Chaconne because it's my piece and Denis' piece and it has to be on the first album.

I had rarely in my life been happier or more fulfilled. Cups of tea and smokes interspersed with people helping me create a record of the music that irreversibly changed my entire fucking galaxy forever. And of course there was the added bonus of the safety net of the retake. I could simply disappear, try new things, take stupid risks with tempos and voicing and sound, listen back, decide what worked and what didn't. I will never, ever forget those few short days where everything on the outside disappeared and all that mattered was the music, the piano, somehow playing notes written two or three hundred years ago by some mad, genius bastard of a composer out of his mind with grief or love or both.

I get home knowing it's going to be a few weeks before I get to hear the first edit. Who cares? I'm playing, working, dreaming, hanging out with my son, seeing my shrink, going to AA meetings. Back on some kind of road that doesn't involve destruction and self-hatred.

And I guess the gods were feeling generous around that time because not only did I get a second chance at the career of my dreams, meet the guy who could help make that happen and find some degree of emotional equilibrium, but I met a girl.

She was not so much a girl. More a tall, slender, shiny, blonde über-girl. One sunny morning I'm finishing up a coffee with my pal Luca (a tiny, chiselled, insanely happy and over-enthusiastic Italian man I'd met a year or two before in one of my many therapy groups), and see her walking towards us. Turns out she's a pal of his and was passing by the café when she saw him in the window and came in to say hello. I've never seen someone so lit up with such a massive fucking dose of prettiness. And when Luca introduces us she lets rip an enormous smile and pulls up a chair.

It had been six months since the separation and I was in the middle of the divorce process. Imagine for a moment what this must feel like for me. I weigh eight stone. My arms are covered with self-inflicted scars. I'm living in a pretty squalid basement flat round the corner from a furious ex-wife. I've got weekend-only access to my son, and no money. I'm a few short months out of a psychiatric hospital, and after all of the emotional fuckery of the past few years spend most of my days in some kind of dreamlike, dissociated fugue state. And this girl, Hattie, is smiling at me and seems interested in who I am. I hadn't been looking for anyone, was pretty sure I was incapable of all but the most basic social skills, was able to focus only on music and looked rancid and wasted and spectral. But I couldn't stop staring at her. Flawless skin, shiny eyes, stupidly gym-toned lithe body, the most seductive mouth I've ever seen, smelling of hope and loveliness. And, much as I hate the phrase, one of the cool kids. You know the kind at parties who draw people to them because they're just so fucking cool they don't even know it, and wherever they stand there's a draught? She was twenty-four, I was thirty-two.

I know.

She was so far out of my league that there was nothing to be scared of. I knew it was never going to happen. So I just smiled, flirted, acted the way I wanted to without ever thinking it would go anywhere. Much the same way as you buy a lottery ticket knowing you'll never win. It's fun to dream.

We swap numbers and I head home, hating her slightly just for being the kind of girl that other girls wanted to be and other guys simply wanted. I fire off the obligatory text about how lovely it was to meet her, maybe we could grab a drink, etc etc, and get back to the piano now hating myself slightly for knocking on a door I knew would be slammed in my face but choosing to do it anyway.

And within an hour she gets back to me. With x's and everything (not even the slightly lazy '<full stop> X' but the '<full stop> xxx' – an important difference, honest). And that moment, that echoey phone beep, that string of random binary data hurtling through the air, deciphered by Nokia and displayed on my screen was, along with the birth of my son, the first note of Bach's Chaconne and meeting Denis the final part of the miraculous quartet that would change my life forever.

Chopin, Fantasie in F minor, Op. 49
Krystian Zimerman, Piano

Chopin wrote his F minor Fantasie when he was on holiday in Spain with his girlfriend, the writer George Sand. It was a dysfunctional, fucked-up, turd of a relationship that pretty much finished him off. This piece, apocryphally at least, opens with Sand knocking at the door and Chopin answering with all the ensuing love, madness, chaos and (occasional) poetry that summed up their fucked-up relationship.

One of my early birthday presents from Hattie was a giant canvas upon which she had transcribed, by hand, the opening couple of pages of this piece, surrounded by beautiful illustrations of flowers and patterns, framed and on the wall.

Cringe all you want.

We're doing so much better than Chopin and Sand ever did.

SHE CAME ROUND TO MY flat the next day. I'd suggested hanging out. She was off out somewhere and was driving right past mine, so she said she could swing by for an hour. I was like a fucking fourteen-year-old, rushing around tidying, checking my hair, my breath, my clothes. And then I stopped and just decided to calm the fuck down, do something crazy like simply be myself, and see what happened. Which lasted all of three minutes before I started rushing around again like an insecure asshole desperate for her to like me. Stupid love. Makes us all act like dickheads.

She came round and we sat on my sofa and smoked and talked, and holy shit it was the best thing ever. I'd never been in awe of someone like this before, at least not someone who seemed to want to hang out with me and wasn't some character on a TV screen. Never been so close to someone who seemed to have this kind of halo of loveliness around them. There was this thing between us. Something almost tangible, something I could feel deep down that wasn't lust or obsession or awkwardness or neediness. It was new and unfamiliar and electric. I see now that I had found someone who fit me perfectly, and even more amazingly, whom I fit too. Her crazy and my crazy seemed to meet in the ether between us and form a solid shape that was unbreakable. It was some kind of fucked-up sexual, spiritual alchemy that neither of us could understand or even identify, but it was there, it was powerful and it was deep enough to make me sound like a massive prick when writing about it.

We started dating. I bought her flowers. It was beautiful, exciting, terrifying, electric, exhausting. Over the first few weeks, the realities of being in a new relationship revealed both of our respective kinks. Funnily enough, she had her own past, as I had mine. She was in many ways the most fragile thing I'd ever met, in other ways the strongest. And that only made me love her more. We were, with our respective weirdness and baggage, like two developmentally stunted kids creating a safe place to get to know one another in a world that still felt slightly overwhelming to both of us. And it was lovely.

And yet . . . The thought that I would be able to function responsibly in a relationship was, in retrospect, pretty laughable. I so did not want to fuck this up. I knew how big a deal it was. Women like this do not come around often. Rushdie said something brilliant about women always choosing, and men, if they're lucky, getting chosen. Oh how I wanted to be chosen. And she did choose me. She chose me every day in every way and I couldn't quite believe it.

I would get deeply insecure and freak out, I'd interpret her desire for closeness and 'talking about feelings' as ambushes and shut down, disappearing if not physically then at least emotionally. I'd push her away, realise that it was nothing to do with her and was simply my shit, beg her to take me back after a week and then start the whole process again, until a few months later when I'd repeat the cycle. I don't know if it's because I was scared of getting close to someone for the first time in my life, or if I was still grieving the breakdown of my family unit and simply could not make room for an intimate relationship. But I do know that I loved her. There was this amazing bond connecting us that never weakened. I wanted her so much, and I knew, for the first time ever and despite knowing what a stupid cliché it is, that this was real love.

We were, however spastically, starting to build our little life together. Jack was coming over every weekend, and he and Hattie clicked into place effortlessly and easily. Perhaps it was because of her own childlike sense of awe (a genuine delight at bright colours, healthy appreciation of fart jokes, a penchant for pulling funny faces and idiotic dancing), but he adored her from the get-go and she him. If you ever need a foolproof test for predicting the longevity of a relationship, see how your lover acts around children. And notice how kids act around him or her – they're smart fuckers and usually there's a good reason if they don't want to go near a certain adult. Jack walked right into her open arms and heart, happily and safely.

As the weeks passed, Jack shuttling back and forth between my home and his mum's, I started becoming concerned about the way our break-up and communication failure would affect Jack. This was one of the worst aspects of the break-up for me – the way that our failure to operate as a functional ex-family would inevitably distress him. We had once had, on paper at least, a picture-perfect family with money, a cute kid, a lovely house, nice things. Then I got sick, broke down, destroyed it all. There was just too much destruction. Should we have stayed together anyway for Jack? Fuck, no, what sort of a message would that have sent him?

I, naively, thought we'd have one of those great divorced-couple relationships where we're buddies, talking about each other's new dates, catching up over coffee once a fortnight. I so desperately hoped she'd find a decent guy, have more career success, live happily. But she wasn't having any of it. She had, understandably and justifiably, had enough. There had been so much destruction, so much uncertainty and pain, and clearly Jane had decided that Jack's needs had to come first. She was a mother first and foremost and not some patron saint of lost causes.

And soon after Hattie and I started dating I got an email from Jane telling me she was going to move to America with Jack.

I spoke to my lawyer. On paper I had no income, no career, no properties, securities, cash or assets. I'd had a chequered mental and emotional history and my son lived 80 per cent of the time with his mother. There was no chance at all I could convince the courts to rule in my favour. At best I could drag things out for a few months, force us both into court and myself into debt and postpone the inevitable. I couldn't see the point.

And so they left to go live in Pittsburgh where they found a home and an amazing school that suited Jack brilliantly. And I was OK for a while. I sold myself the idea that it was for the best, especially for him. I did what I could to get photos, updates, be involved in decisions regarding his schooling and health, regular Skype sessions and visits. It didn't occur to me that once they got there and got settled there would be no photos, barely any updates of any kind. Access would be allowed, but as for the details of his life and upbringing, I felt like I was going to be cut out of the loop. I had pushed her so far for so long that I guess she needed a fresh start and the last thing she wanted to think about was ensuring I was kept up to date with their news,

I am just so grateful she still allowed me access to Jack – many women would not have. He and I Skyped twice a week and I would make the 25-hour door-to-door trip as often as I could, staying in a hotel and trying my best to be solid for him in a very unsolid situation.

I'd leave home, fly out to New York or Boston, wait around for four hours until my connection to Pittsburgh, go straight from the airport in a cab to their house, pick him up, go on to the hotel and spend four or five days with him. The first time I did it was just before Christmas.

Hattie and I were having a break – I'd freaked out and felt, wrongly, that I simply could not deal with acting like an adult in our relationship. I felt smothered, overwhelmed, terrified and immensely sad that my son was 5,000 miles away. And so, of course, my solution was to make sure I was alone. That is my default answer to everything overwhelming – move away from, not towards, those who love me. My sadness would drown her, it would push her away, and so I had to pre-empt that by doing it first. Such stupid fucking arrogance on my part.

I got to Pittsburgh, picked Jack up and off we went to my hotel. It was freezing cold, snowing, miserable. He was now seven years old.

How can anyone find the words to explain to a young child why he lives the other side of the world, away from his father, his friends, his old life? How does one explain that love between adults can sometimes lessen over time but love for a child only grows? How the fuck can someone meet the unassailable, desolate logic of a seven-year-old who cannot fathom why Mum and Dad, even when divorced, can't still live next door to one another with a child-friendly explanation?

It was an unforgettable moment when, at 4 a.m., I was jetlagged and realised I was responsible for everything bad in my son's world.

And then I thought of Hattie back in London, probably dressing up and going out with friends, no doubt getting hit on by guys, maybe even hitting on guys herself, thinking I'd lost her for good, too. And I fell even further down the hole.

I called her. I couldn't not – she was the first, the only, woman who has really seen me. She'd met me after I'd uncovered and worked through all of my shit and so she met the real me, not the set of symptoms or the mask or the carefully crafted lie. I think that's why I was finding the relationship so challenging – I was a total novice at living like this, a beginner at being me, working hard to not slip into a misleading and misguided version of me. And she still loved me, despite seeing what was underneath.

And again, kindness. Her voice was full of reassurance, love, compassion. She told me she would be waiting at Heathrow when I got back. That I just had to get through the next forty-eight hours, take a few cabs, visit a few museums and pizza places, help make some lovely memories for Jack. And I did all of that. And when I got back to England, there she was, waiting at the arrivals gate at six in the morning. With the kindest, gentlest fucking smile I'd ever seen.

We went home, we made tea, we had sex, she let the past go and once again jumped back into our relationship, her heart a little more shaken and a little more fragile as a result of my instability.

I got into some kind of routine with Jack. I'd go over there twice a year, his mum would bring him over here while on business twice a year, we'd Skype twice a week and I'd do my best to focus on other things like Hattie and playing the piano when the pain of his not being here got too much.

Being broke was becoming more and more frustrating. There is little enough money in classical music at the best of times, but there is nothing when starting out from scratch. And transatlantic airfares, divorce lawyers, shrinks and rent all added up to something nausea-inducing. I'd quite randomly met a guy called David Tang a few years previously when I was considering becoming an agent. He is a loud, frightening, brilliant, astonishingly kind Hong-Kong-born gazillionaire. We'd met because I'd heard he was a fan of Sokolov, and I figured he'd potentially be a good guy to know should I want to start my own agency up. So I found his address and dropped off a bunch of private recordings of Sokolov I'd got from his manager that I knew he wouldn't have. He called the next day, sent his Bentley and driver round to pick me up and take me round to his house for tea, and then a few days later flew me to Venice with him to see Sokolov play at La Fenice as a thank you.

Most people send a card.

I called him and met him for coffee and, in my typically manipulative way, let him know I was struggling, that I didn't want to throw in the towel and return to the City just yet, and could he help. And he did. Without even really discussing it, he simply called his personal banker then and there and set up a monthly standing order into my account. Like he was ordering a coffee at Starbucks.

I wouldn't be here were it not for him. And even if by some miracle I were still here, I most certainly would not be playing the piano. His cash paid for medical bills, Billy and other shrinks, a better piano, it bought me time and space to practise, kept my head vaguely gentle and allowed me to focus on what I needed to. It was a rare, incredible thing to have done for me. He thought I played well, wanted to help out, did not ask for anything in return, and for that difficult first eighteen months post-divorce made everything possible. Some things can never be repaid, at least not quickly. There will come a time when

I pay him back every dime. There will, I hope, come a time when I perform the same act of kindness for someone else. Right now though I can only think about what he has done for me, slack-jawed with disbelief at his generosity, and try my hardest not to let him down. Sometimes I feel like I am the luckiest man I know.

Ravel, Piano Concerto in G, Second Movement

Krystian Zimerman, Piano

Ravel composed two piano concertos. One of them was written for the left hand alone (it was commissioned by Paul Wittgenstein, an Austrian pianist who lost his right arm during the First World War) and the other one was written after a tour of America where he had encountered the world of jazz – the whole work is heavily influenced by swing and smoke-infested Harlem jazz clubs.

It took him two years to complete and contains arguably the most beautiful slow movement of any concerto ever written. I remember as a kid reading an interview with someone (frustratingly I don't remember who, only that he was a vicar or something similar) who was asked the question: if the end of the world were coming and you were given a ten-minute warning, what would you do? He replied that he'd pour a glass of very expensive scotch and listen to this piece of music.

Ravel sweated blood working on each note of this concerto. (To a friend he wrote, 'The G-major Concerto took two years of work, you know. The opening theme came to me on a train between Oxford and London. But the initial idea is nothing. The work of chiselling then began. We've gone past the days when the composer was thought of as being struck by inspiration, feverishly scribbling down his thoughts on a scrap of paper. Writing music is seventy-five per cent an intellectual activity.' And of the second movement he said, 'That flowing phrase! How I worked over it bar by bar! It nearly killed me!'

It contains everything that cements his reputation as one of France's supreme musical geniuses − extraordinary melodies, flawless orchestration, a depth of feeling that beggars belief.

I WAS BUILDING SOMETHING THRILLING, if as yet indefinable, with Hattie, learning the hard way that life without self-destructing is difficult, long-distance fatherhood is not a walk in the park, and for the first time in my life, daring to dream that a career doing what I'd always loved more than anything else was, at least potentially, workable.

I threw myself even more deeply into the piano, learning new pieces, honing my technique, preparing, preparing, preparing. The first album was ready, having gone through the editing process. We decided to call it *Razor Blades, Little Pills and Big Pianos*. It was autobiographical enough to define most of my life in seven words and hopefully sounded different enough to get noticed by the music press. Ditto for the artwork − if I see another fucking eighteenth-century French watercolour or a photo of some awkward, gurning pianist on a classical album cover I'll eat my own face. We managed to convince Dennis Morris, who had been for a time Bob Marley's official photographer and worked with the Sex Pistols, to take the snaps, and the finished album looked so far removed from the typical classical album that a few classical reviewers thought it had landed on the wrong desk. One journalist from the US even said there were so many pictures of me in my Ray-Bans that he thought I was blind. Which I was quite proud of. Again, why the fuck not? Why not have some album art that stands out, looks vaguely current, has a greater chance of appealing to first-time classical listeners, and wouldn't automatically stop a girl from making out with you if she saw it on your coffee table?

So I had my very own CD out in the shops. And it didn't involve me recording myself on a shitty MP3 player, burning it to disc and printing out a wanky homemade cover using my computer as I'd done somewhat shamefully in the past. Ego aside, it was a big moment for me and felt like a huge first step in a career I'd been dreaming about since I was a kid.

In 2010, a few months after *Razor Blades* came out, the BBC approached Denis and me to do a documentary about Chopin for his bicentenary. It was my first TV gig, and a genuinely thrilling experience. I travelled to Poland, saw Chopin's birthplace, the house where he spent his teenage years, the tomb where they keep his heart, the piano he used to compose on. We went to Paris and did midnight shoots in the Place Vendôme, improvising pieces to camera. I interviewed legendary pianists Emanuel Ax and Garrick Ohlsson *at the piano* and got all excited. We filmed a couple of concerts of mine where I was playing Chopin and the whole thing was pretty much the most fun I could have had without involving narcotics. I knew then that TV was something I really wanted to focus on. Of course it was. Editing could make me sound semi-articulate, I was being paid to talk about things I couldn't shut up about in the first place, and I got to meet my heroes and travel around the world.

By now Denis had started to get some bigger concerts lined up: one at the Queen Elizabeth Hall, where I'd seen most of my child-hood heroes play, from Sokolov to Zimerman to Brendel, and one at the Roundhouse, where everyone from Pink Floyd to Jimi Hendrix had played.

He and I were chatting over coffee one morning about these concerts. Piano recitals followed a hallowed and strict format. White tie and tails for the performer (or at the very least a suit/tuxedo). No talking. Walk on stage, play, leave. The audience had programme notes, the hall lights were up pretty high so they could read them during the performance, no drinks were allowed, clapping between movements of pieces was frowned upon, the audience was expected to know enough about the music to 'get it'.

'Do you remember that first time you played to me at Steinway Hall – the Chaconne?' he asked me.

'Of course I do – the best time ever!'

'Well I was thinking about that. How you were jabbering away about the piece, about Bach, about what it meant to you, then you just sat and played it, then you bounced up and started talking about coffee as if you'd just done something totally pedestrian. And I was still reeling from an all-out emotional assault, and I was thinking, what if we made our concert like that?

'You introduce the pieces, talk about the composers, chat to the audience between each piece. You do it in your own words, not through some Oxford don's essay in the programme, you wear what you want, we keep the lights right down, we make it more of an immersive, informal experience. Whaddya think?'

They say that every good idea starts out as a blasphemy. Thing is, this sounded perfect to me. Christ, how I wished I could have heard any of the pianists I'd seen when I was going to concerts as a kid actually talking to us in the audience. The thought of Kissin or Zimerman or Richter talking about why they had chosen to play that particular Beethoven sonata, what it meant to them, would have been meteorically cool. The classical music industry caters to a fraction of a percentage of the population, especially in the UK. It is run by, for the most part, pompous, archaic wankers who seem to take a perverse kind of pleasure in keeping 'proper' music as the privilege of an elite few who they deem wealthy enough (and therefore intelligent enough) to understand it. Beethoven is their posh fucking house and the only people they want to invite in are those who know which fork to use with the fish course and the difference between Köchel numbers and opus numbers.

There are just so many issues, complications and difficulties with classical music. As a genre it seems to have become the musical equivalent of cranking – crying while wanking because you're so ashamed of what it is you're thinking about. Classical music has to stop apologising for itself. The problems need to be identified and accepted, rehab style, before there is any hope of permanent change.

First and foremost, the name. Classical. Why? As I mentioned at the beginning of this book, it gives the impression of something outdated, irrelevant, passé, inaccessible and above all, boring. Is a new *Lear* production called classical theatre? Do we go to visit an exhibition at a classical art gallery? Do we fuck. Music somehow insists on segregating itself. Classical radio stations, classical concerts, classical composers, classical music magazines, classical CD departments, classical musicians. Feel free to substitute the world 'classical' for highbrow, intelligent, worthy, more profound. Most of the people involved in the classical music world act as if it is all of those things anyway.

The other big problem with this bizarre, eclectic and locked-in world is, of course, the people involved, the majority of whom put the 'ass' into 'classical'. These fall into four distinct categories: performers, gatekeepers, record label execs and critics. As with any generalisations, there are a few exceptions to what follows, people in the industry who have a genuine love for music and a desire to make it vibrant and accessible. But anyone looking at my industry from the outside would see the vast majority of those inside it as follows:

a) The performers. Usually socially retarded and extremely awkward. Almost invariably on the Asperger's/autism scale (as am I – not a criticism but it can make us hard to engage with). Dubious and scary taste in clothing (either paedophile sweaters or ill-fitting white tie and tails). Emotionally castrated, either asexual or massively camp, serial-killer weird, mumbling lunatics with a higher than average number of sexual fetishes. No doubt highly intelligent but virtually incapable of normal social interaction. At concerts they appear, play and leave. Mingling with the audience is an extremely rare event and usually only at the behest of the record label (see below) who demand a CD signing post-concert. Talking to the audience (beyond the occasional encore title delivered in a monotone) is almost unheard of. These guys (and girls), perhaps more than anybody else, have only themselves to blame for the state of classical music today. Social anxiety is often a mask for ego – refusing to play in venues that aren't prestigious enough, point-blank refusal to engage with fans and audiences, a general attitude of 'leave me alone with my own genius because that should be enough to make it'. Well it ain't. Not any more.

b) Gatekeepers. These guys (99 per cent male, white, old) are the ones who run the concert halls and agencies. In recent times, due to dwindling, dying audiences and cuts in public funding, they have been forced to bleat on about opening up the doors to a younger and fresher audience but in reality have done absolutely fuck all to achieve this beyond empty gestures that they deem would be down with the kids like occasional late night concerts and using slightly different fonts in their brochures. For the most part they sit on the fence, drinking champagne with and sweet-talking wealthy older patrons operating under the assumption that all change is monstrously bad, that having a younger audience would be catastrophic for the industry and that their hall/orchestra/institution is doing perfectly well as it is, thank you very much. It's like Bernie Madoff's mum whistling bravely in the dark in the unshakeable belief that the whole thing is an awful misunderstanding and that her cash is definitely safe and nothing bad is going to happen.

The most despicable part of this for me is their assumption that new, younger audiences would somehow cheapen the classical music world. God forbid someone turns up wearing jeans and dares to applaud in the 'wrong' place. That unless you are an OBE, MA, MSc, Oxbridge-educated, £80,000+ earning, Windsor-knot wearing parody of yourself you are going to detract from the immaculate, refined, ultra-fragile and culturally sacred world that is classical music. Go to any 'established' concert hall in the UK and you will see an audience comprising 10 per cent music students, 85 per cent over-fifties fulfilling one or several of the above criteria, and 5 per cent decent, ordinary music fans with no pretensions and a genuine love for classical music. (This paragraph reads as such a cliché because it's still so true.)

c) Record labels. The (invariably) small, ashamed, naive labels run by well-meaning, meek types with not a shred of business acumen and no desire to even try anything different. Purveyors of dull, lazy album covers and promotional posters (artists looking constipated/French watercolours/abstract scenes in muted colours/Lang Lang with fingers painted as piano keys, for fuck's sake); sleeve notes written by academics who've written books on eighteenth-century sonata form; a marketing budget of £30; a lazy willingness to settle for being placed amongst thousands of other similar products in the basement of HMV where you need a head torch and absolutely no sense of shame to enter; a label president (who doubles as A&R, marketing, photocopier and fluffer) for whom making a phone call to iTunes/HMV/Amazon and asking for any kind of promotion/cross-marketing deal is as alien as Pol Pot adopting a rescue puppy. These guys are slowly but surely draining the lifeblood out of the business and have been for years. There are, thank God, a couple of notable exceptions who are breaking new ground and taking a few risks that five years ago would have resulted in them being stoned to death.

The classical offshoots of the major labels (Sony Classical, DG, WCJ etc) are perhaps the saddest of all. Most of them have been booted out of the main HQs and relegated to scummy industrial parks with a staff of three, a budget frozen year after year, a veto on new signings and the shame of being the major label's little brother who turned out to be a serial granny rapist. Ignored and laughed at by their major rock division big brothers, they survive on a back catalogue that harks back to the golden age of the 1950s and '60s.

The apparently easy solution for them is crossover. To take a group of hot young things, dress them up, have them play a combination of short, famous passages from longer works and transcriptions of 'Waltzing Matilda', *The Phantom of the Opera* etc and hope, desperately, that people will buy the lie that this is 'classical music' and part with their cash.

d) Critics. The lonely, embittered, failed musician, asshole-disguised-as-academic dickhead. The epitome of all that is wrong with classical music today. The sneering, snobbish, ill-informed and vicious ranters who would not be taken seriously in any other kind of journalistic endeavour and gleefully whore out their copy at 25p per word to the few people willing to pay attention. The majority of classical music critics should be looked on as angry, overweight kids who have somehow survived years of bullying, have long ago given up their dreams of doing something creative and worthwhile and now insist on boring to death anyone who will listen (basically other critics, senile classical audiences, the odd music student and a few high court judges).

Clearly there are major problems in the music world. A blinkered outlook by the majority of those in positions of influence, a childish refusal born largely of fear and conservatism to attempt to reach a broader audience, a desperate clinging to what's familiar despite over-whelming evidence that they are on a sinking ship, a horror of and immediate lashing out at anyone who dares to try new things with old music, and most depressingly, a greedy, grasping desire to keep this incredible music just for themselves and a select few who fit their criteria as worthy listeners.

The people behind classical music seem to have lost sight of the fact that the composers themselves were, in effect, the original rock stars. Today the phrase 'rock star' brings to mind *Heat* magazine photo-shoots, tattoos, wanky phrases like 'conscious uncoupling', being a judge on *Britain's Got Talent*. Back then it meant really bad hair, some form of venereal disease, mental illness and poverty. They were for the large part mental, depraved, genius bastards who would have pissed themselves laughing at the ideas about performance that the classical gatekeepers of today are so rigidly stuck to. They didn't throw TVs out of hotel windows, they threw themselves out.

Beethoven moved house seventy times. He was clumsy, badly coordinated, couldn't dance, cut himself while shaving. He was sullen, suspicious, touchy, incredibly messy and angry. And he went on to change the course of musical history. In 1805 he wrote the 'Eroica' Symphony, and with one compulsive wrench, music entered the nineteenth century. While every other composer was trying to woo their audience, he kicked down doors and planted bombs under their seats. The idea of forcing his audience to sit in silence, without applauding during pieces, would have made him laugh like a drain.

Schubert, nicknamed 'Little Mushroom' on account of his being 5 foot nothing and violently ugly, was spectacularly unsuccessful with girls and, on one of the very rare occasions he did manage to score, he caught syphilis. A friend of his said, 'How powerfully the craving for pleasure dragged his soul down to the slough of moral degradation.' Schubert, by his own admission, came into the world 'for no purpose other than to compose', and he earned the equivalent in today's money of around £7,000 (in total) in the last twelve years of his life, with less than 10 per cent of his output published in his lifetime. He was broke, oversensitive, lost his hair, lived in squats, and led a life of relentlessly, miserable drudgery. Would he give a fuck about whether his music was played with the performers or audience wearing the right attire?

From Schumann (who died alone and miserable in a mental asylum) to Ravel (whose experiences driving trucks and ambulances in the First World War changed him forever), the great composers were basket-case geniuses, and were they to come to the average concert today and see the prices, audiences, presentation and pretension surrounding their music, they would be fucking disgusted.

No wonder I was so desperate to do it differently.

How lucky I have been to have found a manager who is on the same page. He became a director now as well as a manager. A few days before the Roundhouse gig we went down to Steinway and I ran through the whole programme from start to finish, talking about Bach, Beethoven, Chopin, the pieces, why, when, how. It detracted slightly from the absolute focus of playing just the notes, but not enough to make it non-viable. I just had to concentrate a little bit harder, remember a few more things and try not to say anything too inappropriate.

Concert day arrived and I pitched up to the hall. There were eight cameras positioned around the auditorium with a keyboard cam for good measure and two giant screens on stage. The idea was that we would relay a live video from different angles while I was playing. That way people in the cheap seats could see everything clearly, and in all the really tricky passages I'd spent thousands of hours working on, everyone could see my hands in close-up, because it looks awesome and I'm quite vain.

It was an incredibly intense experience. It was clear from the feedback afterwards that the majority of the audience had never been to a classical concert before and the average age of the audience was mid to late twenties, a far cry from the usual fifty-plus Wigmore Hall crowd. I introduced all the pieces, talked about the composers' back stories, played my heart out and then wanted to do the whole thing over again.

I remember as a kid seeing videos of Glenn Gould chatting to the audience in Moscow and Bernstein talking from the stage before conducting masterpiece after masterpiece, but in recent memory I don't think anyone had ever talked at length and played in a classical concert before other than Daniel Barenboim who talked briefly about Schoenberg from the podium at the Festival Hall a few years ago (it was such a break from tradition it made the newspapers). And cracking the odd joke, sharing anecdotes about Bach fighting and fucking, about Beethoven being almost beaten to death by his drunken father, and talking about why I wanted to play these specific pieces seemed to work well. Having an audience applaud the speaking as well as the playing, and hearing laughter in a classical concert seemed to confirm that this was a good direction to be moving in. I was finally doing what I had dreamed about doing forever. I had never felt so fulfilled in all my life.

And a couple of weeks later we did the exact same thing, minus the screens, at the QEH. Again, a young audience, bemused expressions from the backstage tech crew who had never had to mike up a classical performer before, laughter, music, low lighting, absolute silence from the audience while I was playing, hanging out in the bar afterwards with some of the guys who'd come down to listen. It was, for me, the perfect way to give a concert. It removed the bullshit and ego surrounding so much of the classical music industry and yet stayed true to why we do this job in the first place – the music.

There are so many fucking rules in place around classical music: the dress code, performance practice, programme notes, lighting, presentation, concert format, applause, repertoire choice, timing, performer and audience etiquette, venue choice, and on and on.

Denis and I have only ever had two rules: no crossover ever (not because I'm against it as a genre but because it just doesn't do it for me when there is so much classical music out there already), and no dumbing down the music (in many ways the same thing). Everything else was fair game and the gloves were off. So if I found out one of my concerts wasn't totally sold out I'd tell Denis to offer the remaining tickets for free, because why the hell shouldn't we offer a few people the chance of a free night of music? Luckily, and to the joy of my promoters, things are now at a place where I don't have to do that any more. But the point is, was, always will be, to fill 'em up, choose music that is immortal and accessible, play as well as I can, talk about music, wear clothes that are comfortable and not based on the performance practice of the 1930s, let the audience bring drinks in, turn the lighting down to almost pitch black. Make it immersive, intimate, exciting and informative. Rip up the rule book and just do what feels right.

We were definitely starting as we meant to go on. It was difficult and frustrating trying to find like-minded people in the industry who were open to looking at and presenting classical in a different way. I knew that there would always be an audience for the immortal pianists of this world like Kissin, Zimerman, Argerich, as well there should be. But much more importantly, I knew that there must be at least forty-five million people in the UK alone who had never heard a Beethoven sonata in its entirety before, and that was something I found deeply depressing. It wasn't about preaching to the converted, or even preaching at all, to anyone. It was simply about reaching as many people as possible with something that perhaps they hadn't yet heard, and doing it in a way that made it accessible and comfortable for everyone. There was no mission involved – serial killers go on missions – but it felt urgent and important and true, and other than Hattie, there wasn't much of that going on in my life at that point.

We started to get a fair bit of press interest both good and bad. There was some douchebag in the *Daily Telegraph* who started off his piece saying he'd never heard of me, never heard me play, never been to any of my concerts or heard my album, but that I was an arrogant prick who was trying to 'save' classical music by wearing trainers and jeans when it was doing very well on its own, thank you very much, etc etc. We knew this was going to happen, especially with the old-school classical brigade. What was unexpected, and rather lovely, was the number of really great reviews I got for the album and concerts. I know the goal is to be immune to both criticism and praise, but I'm human, and all of that stuff affects me. I call bullshit on anyone who says it doesn't. Especially those of us who feel like giant frauds in the first place and disbelieve kind comments while absolutely knowing the negative ones are true.

If you're somebody for whom the idea of going to a piano recital appeals about as much as a trip to the dentist, maybe consider coming to one of mine. Bring a date, know that it will be casual, inclusive, that the music will be immense. And if I'm not your cup of tea then try the Wigmore or Festival Hall. Go see Stephen Hough, Daniil Trifonov, or any one of a hundred A-game pianists on the circuit right now. Investigate something new and see where it leads. To experience music like this live is something extraordinary.

I was, for the first time in a long time, in a really good place both emotionally and physically. A kind, beautiful girlfriend, a dedicated, genius manager, concerts and music at the centre of my world, slowly increasing odds that the career of my dreams could actually happen. And a growing sense of acceptance that Jack was in another country coupled with the hope that he and I could still maintain some kind of relationship.

Schumann, 'Geister Variations' for Piano

Jean–Marc Luisada, Piano

Composers and mental illness go hand in hand like Catholics and guilt, or America and obesity. Schumann was one of several who suffered from severe depression, throwing himself into the Rhine and then, having not managed to kill himself, sectioning himself voluntarily and dying alone and afraid in an asylum.

Days before he tried to kill himself he wrote his 'Geister (Ghost) Variations', so called because he said that ghosts had dictated the opening theme to him. Yep. Slightly unhinged.

There is not a more private, enclosed, intense, concentrated piano composition that I can think of. Rarely rising above a forte, the theme is a chorale that slowly, gently develops into something far beyond words. Here is Schumann's schizophrenic, depressed, lost world laid bare at our feet.

AMONGST ALL THE PRESS THAT was starting to happen at that time, I did an interview in the *Sunday Times*. In it I mentioned the sexual abuse that had happened at school – it was a short paragraph in a double-page piece. The head of the junior school from back then saw it and got in touch with me (Facebook is good for some things, apparently). She told me she'd known that some kind of abuse was happening (even if, in her naivety, she hadn't thought it was sexual), that she used to find me sobbing, blood on my legs, begging not to go back to gym class. She'd gone to the head of the school who'd said, in true 1980s style, 'Little Rhodes needs to toughen up. Ignore it.' Which she did. She told me that she quit her job and became a prison chaplain. And then years later read my interview and got in touch to see if she could put things right. Twenty-five years too fucking late, but hey ho. Slightly angry about that still.

She made a police statement (the one I included earlier in this book). I went back to the police with my manager once they'd received it and we tried again. He may have mentioned press coverage and record label lawyers. And sure enough they found the guy. He was in his seventies. And working in Margate. As a part-time boxing coach for boys under ten.

After lengthy interviews, they arrested him and charged him with ten counts of buggery and indecent assault.

And so when some people let me know that I'm only talking about the abuse that happened as a means of selling albums or getting sympathy (it happens), I always tell them that story and ask them if they'd rather I'd kept quiet about the sexual abuse and that guy was still coaching their eight-year-old nephew/son/grandson. Dicks.

The last I heard from the Met police was that he had had a stroke and was deemed unfit to stand trial. He died shortly after I got that news. Many of the books I've read and support groups I've been to talk about forgiveness. They suggest writing letters to those who have hurt us, especially if they are no longer alive, outlining the impact of their actions on ourselves and on those we love. And in many ways that is what this book is. It is my letter to you, Peter Lee, as you rot in your filthy grave, letting you know that you haven't yet won. Our secret is no longer a secret, a bond we share, a private, intimate connection to you of any kind. No part of anything you did to me was harmless, enjoyable or loving, despite what you said. It was simply an abhorrent, penetrative violation of innocence and trust.

I can but hope that people like Mr Lee, people who actively pursue and engage in their sexual desire for children see, really see, the damage it does. That passing it off or justifying it as mutual and acceptable, an expression of love, is as far from the truth as it is possible to get.

Forgiveness is a glorious concept. It's something I aspire to even if it's at times seemingly nothing more than an impossible, if desirable, fantasy. There have been too many incidents of abuse in my life. I am committed to sharing the parts of it that I'm able to cope with without totally imploding. And that's good enough for me. It has to be. There are other people from my past who know more and should have known better and they will have to make their peace with that just as I am trying to. Maybe one day I will forgive Mr Lee. That's much likelier to happen if I find a way to forgive myself. But the truth, for me at any rate, is that the sexual abuse of children rarely, if ever, ends in forgiveness. It leads only to self-blame, visceral, self-directed rage and shame.

The sexual abuse of children.

Some people read that phrase and feel appalled, some feel titillated, some feel angry, some turned on. It's interesting to see that just by writing that phrase I want to disappear for a while and do something destructive, distractive, anything to avoid these feelings. Thirty years later I'm still right there, pinned down and in pain and feeling like it was all my fault. Just because I've written a few words about it. The inherent power of this shit to fuck you up with nothing more than a sideways sneer is terrifying.

When the Jimmy Savile case reared its ugly head I was asked to write a piece for the *Daily Telegraph* about it. Somehow by this time I'd managed to find a voice and some kind of status in the media that allowed me to talk about things like this in the hope of adding, in some small way, to the changes that are already happening since more people started talking about it. The full article is in the Appendix to this book, and writing it spun me out for a few weeks afterwards because, well, it's giving oxygen to something that really wants to just curl away in the darkness and gnaw away at my insides.

But shining a light on topics like this is hugely important. And getting hundreds of supportive and grateful messages from people who had also gone through similar experiences was an indicator to me that it needs to be talked about even more.

★

Denis and I had made a small start on my musical career. An album, a bit of press, a few concerts. We had some good ideas, and we were lucky enough to have GHP, the touring company that looked after

Stomp since the beginning, get involved, helping secure both classical and non-classical venues. It was enough to keep me busy, but despite being on a more even keel, there were still regular moments each day filled with panic – fear of failure, of an almost empty concert diary, the horror that I had committed everything to becoming a concert pianist and it could, at any minute, fall apart and end up in abject failure. The thing is that I used to feel the exact same way when I worked in the City, served burgers in Burger King, showed up to any job. I am preconditioned and hard-wired to fear the worst, believe every negative voice in my head and expect terrible things to happen. That's just the way it is. On the plus side it keeps me alert, hungry, working hard. On the negative, well, I'm mental, stressed, heinously jealous of others' success.

We also went back to the studio with my little motley crew of engineers and producers to record album number two, *Now Would All Freudians Please Stand Aside*. This was from one of my favourite Glenn Gould quotes. Gould, that musical freak who couldn't have given less of a fuck what people thought of him or his playing. He played Bach like no one before or after could ever hope to, graced the cover of *Time*, had his performances put on the Voyager spacecraft as an example to alien life forms of just how awesome the human race can be, and died of a massive stroke in 1982, no doubt helped along by his epic addiction to prescription drugs. He retired from performing in public at a stupidly young age because he felt the audience was always hostile, waiting for him to screw up. He dedicated the rest of his life to the recording studio, believing (rightly as it turned out) that there was a huge future in recording and massive advances being made in the technology behind it. He worshipped the security of the recording studio and how safe it felt, and after recording five albums I still absolutely agree with him. Some of the most rewarding, distracting, immersive hours I've spent have been in the studio.

Gould was also a certified nutjob. He wore thick overcoats, hats and scarves in the middle of summer, poured boiling water over his hands and forearms before playing, took pills like they were gum drops, called his friends (and strangers) at three in the morning and talked at them even while they slept, played the stock market, hated company, was the closest thing classical has ever had to a rock star. He was also movie-star hot when he was younger. And he played the piano like a god. I'm pretty certain that one of his two seminal Goldberg albums has graced more lists of 'desert island discs' than any other classical recording.

For *Freudians* I decided to do another mixed recital programme. I've never been a huge fan of dedicating an entire album to a single composer, especially when trying to reach a fresh audience. Choice is always good, and Bach, Beethoven, Chopin are my holy trinity. Having Mike Hatch working his magic with sound and microphones, and the genius producer John West (sadly no longer with us thanks to the great fuck that is cancer), made it easier than I deserved. The guys behind the music never get enough credit, and these chaps were absolute experts at polishing my distinctly dodgy attempts into something halfway decent.

Freudians remains the favourite of my recordings and the one I'm most proud of, perhaps because it contains two of music's greatest masterpieces, Beethoven's Op. 109 Sonata and Bach's Sixth Partita.

And we also chose to put a few interviews on the album with me talking about the pieces and the recording process, hopefully without the indulgent wankiness that is so easy to slip into when talking about (LA accent) 'my creative process'.

Here's the thing about careers. We have become so enamoured of and used to the whole 'overnight success' thing promoted by *X Factor* and *Britain's Got Talent* and their ilk that it's easy to feel that success isn't happening fast enough. God knows there were – still are – times when I wish things were moving quicker in my career. And then I look at successful friends of mine whom I admire – Benedict Cumberbatch was doing bit parts in *Heartbeat* and too many unnoticed theatre productions for over a decade before *Sherlock*; Derren Brown was slogging his way through close-up magic in Bristol nightclubs for much longer than that before his career exploded.

I have an in-built terror that good things will slip away. That unless I control things and drive them and micromanage and obsess and worry and push and chase, they will not happen. And there is nothing so destructive to a career as that. It may bring about short-term gain but it is not sustainable – you come across as a giant cock, and no one wants to work with you.

The hardest lesson I've learned is to relax and simply enjoy what is happening today, trusting that if I'm doing the right thing then the right things will happen in their own time. To the point where I'm now very wary of overnight success. I don't think it lasts and, a bit like relationships, there may be a very intense, passionate affair with amazing sex and obscene doses of brain chemicals involved, but chances are it ain't going to be sustained. But taking things slowly, relaxing into it, learning as you go along, enjoying the journey – all of these things build a foundation that can last a lifetime.

I got an inkling of this when I signed to Warner Bros Records. *Freudians* had been released and had had good reviews, I'd been playing around London and in the big festivals – Cheltenham, Hay, Latitude – writing for the *Telegraph* about everything from Formula One (the greatest sport in the world) to Twitter to Beethoven, and generally plugging away at things. I was introduced to Stephen Fry around this time, too.

We'd met through my benefactor, sponsor and supporter Sir David Tang. He had called me up to invite me to a concert and asked me to meet him in the bar at Claridge's Hotel for a drink beforehand. He told me Stephen Fry was coming too and would be there. So off I toddle and of course I'm an hour early as per usual. And sitting in the bar is Fry drinking a martini. He seems startled when I introduce myself until I tell him I'm a friend of Sir David's and am coming to the concert with them and he relaxes a bit and invites me to join him. I ask him what he's been up to, which is unlike me as I usually just start talking about myself, and he tells me he's just finished a series on endangered species and has been in New Zealand or Zanzibar or somewhere. And I, being nervous, a bit of a dick, attention-hungry, say to him:

'Dude, who the fuck cares about some web-footed fucking platypus in the arse end of nowhere? Why not focus on helping those closer to home, or real human beings who are starving, fucked, miserable and alone? Jesus. Give me a fucking break.'

He just looked at me, slightly astonished, and tried to answer me. We got into a huge argument within a minute of meeting one another, me refusing to back down and feeling all smug and self-important, him being as civil as was possible under the circumstances. And we kept our distance from then on for the rest of the evening and, feeling embarrassed and slightly ashamed, I took the easier option of thinking he was a bit of a wanker, told him so, and did my best to ignore him.

And then I get home and as I walk through the door I get a text: 'James it was so wonderful meeting you – you are such a lovely man. Ditch the cynicism – it doesn't suit you and life will be so much easier without it, lots of love, Stephen xxx.'

What a dude. There are a tiny handful of people in my life who are able, consistently, to meet my crazy with kindness. He is one of them.

So he and I became buddies and started hanging out some. And he came to one of my concerts at the Proud Galleries in Camden. It was all north London chic with cool paintings, exposed brick, Cutler and Gross glasses and immaculately trimmed beards. They'd brought in a lovely Steinway and I played well enough. Stupidly I also chose to play some Alkan as I knew he was one of Fry's favourite composers and I wanted his approval (I still do). Alkan was a giant cunt. The guy wrote almost impossibly difficult music. And yet I got through it, more thanks to adrenaline than talent, and it all went down pretty well. Stephen then tweeted that I had kicked 'monumental ass', and somewhere in west London, unknown to me, Conrad Withey, one of the big guns at Warner Bros UK saw his tweet and started listening to my records.

Within a few months Denis and I had been approached to sign a deal with Warners on their rock label. This was, at the time, a really big thing. They have a substantial and highly regarded classical label, Warner Classics & Jazz, but the idea of being on the rock label while sticking to core classical music was amazing to me. Finally we could start chipping away at the ghettoisation of classical music, get some proper marketing behind us (I mean these guys had Muse and Metallica on their books, for fuck's sake) and really start to make progress.

We went into the studio to record album number three, *Bullets and Lullabies*. The concept was two discs, one fast, one slow; one to wake up to and one to pass out to. Denis had spent a few years working as a DJ and he loved the idea of making a kind of classical set list that created a sort of storyline comprised of multiple pieces. What was so cool for me was recording little-known and absolutely amazing composers like Alkan, Blumenfeld and Moszkowski alongside Chopin and Beethoven. I really thought this was it – the big break everyone talks about. The album sounded great, the artwork looked brilliant (thanks to the stupendous talent of Dave Brown of *Mighty Boosh* fame), I was getting invites to the Q Awards and sent free clothing and I very quickly fell into the whole trap of being a giant fame-hungry tosser and believing all the egotistical bullshit about being special.

A few months after the album was released we were approached by Sky Arts who wanted to make a series about classical music but without the habitual stuffiness. The head of Warners had liaised with them and it seemed like a great way to move further into the realm of television. It led to seven episodes of a show called *Piano Man* – each one focusing on a particular theme, either one big piece of music or a group of shorter connected pieces, again with introductions, me chatting about the pieces, with awesome on-screen, MTV-style graphics, and yet playing resolutely core classical repertoire, no voice-overs during the performance, absolute focus on the music itself. The production company who made it was Fresh One, Jamie Oliver's company, and it was the start of a hugely productive and enjoyable relationship with a terrific team of people. Having been around a little bit longer now, I can see just how lucky I was to work with a company so hands-on and supportive from the start – I love them hard.

Alas the bosses of both Warner Bros and Sky Arts seemed to think the other would take responsibility for the promotion of the show (no one wants to spend money unless they have to) and a bit like a retarded game of chicken, neither one budged first. Denis was in that initial meeting and begged them to work together to help make this show count. He reiterated that this was classical music and not rock, and because of that they were going to have to throw everything they could at it to make it work. It was a big ask, especially from Warners, who were more accustomed to working with hugely successful bands and a genre of music that was in less need of resurrection than classical.

It was huge fun to film, even if only sixty-three people ended up seeing it, and it gave me a glimpse of what could be achieved with this kind of music, a great director and a decent budget. The whole team somehow managed to take a style of music few people were interested in and show it off in a way that stripped away the bullshit and retained what was important – the music itself. And to be fair, *Piano Man* seems to have made it round the globe pretty successfully – I'm still getting incredibly kind messages in various exotic languages about it. And, if you're curious, it's available on Amazon at a steal.

And then Warners sat me and Denis down and told us that they had got me onto the Royal Variety Show, where literally fifteen million people were going to watch me play live in front of the Queen, and my head exploded. No wonder they weren't so keen to spend a lot of money pushing the Sky Arts show – this would do the job for them, and then some.

Everyone got very excited, we all talked about the tours afterwards, the huge CD sales, the O2 Arena and magazine covers. And all the time, Denis, always awesome, always careful, always realistic, was saying (not just to me but also to Warners) 'What if it doesn't happen?', 'What's plan B?' and, to me, 'Are you sure you're ready for this if it happens?' They, and I, assured him I was and that it was a done deal. To the point that they announced it on their website, I told all my family and friends, and I could think of nothing else.

And of course, the director and producer of the show came to meet me at Steinway a few days before the show was due to happen and they told us they had decided to have less of a focus on classical music this year and go with another genre.

My ego was furious. And I was so ashamed, having told so many friends (who invariably didn't care a bit). But thank God. The thought of having to handle that level of exposure back in 2010 terrifies me.

I would never have made it, and would likely have ended up falling apart, talking to myself and twitching.

Denis and I regrouped, carried on doing what we were doing. I showed up at the piano every day as usual having learned to ignore apparent good news, not listen to hype and conjecture, simply focus on what's in front of me and doing the best job I can do.

He and I were still the entire team despite the odd accusation that we had a massive group of PR people on board. The truth was much more fun – Denis and me, cigarettes, endless coffees and my kitchen table. Of course we had some help along the way from some amazing people – Glynis Henderson at GHP, Simon Millward at Albion Media (Signum's PR company), John Kelleher and Conrad Withey from Warners, but ultimately it was, and still is, me and Denis hanging out, mouthing off, coming up with new ideas, figuring out our way and praying that things are going to work out for the best. Small is beautiful.

He and I saw that the whole music industry had been falling down for a while, that kids weren't paying money for things any more and the days of sitting back and counting on massive profits for minimal work were over. We were totally committed to trying new things, doing things differently.

We must have been doing something right, because the head of the British Phonographic Industry set up a meeting with us to ask me to be a spokesperson for them, railing against music piracy. Which is just about the stupidest thing I ever heard. And I told them so. Why the fuck would people *not* steal music when the whole industry had fucked them up the ass for decades and was too lazy to do its job?

Because the labels were asking them nicely not to? I told them that once they could find a way to give the fans a reason to pay for music, then they would. Willingly and happily. The labels just needed to up their game considerably and not feel entitled to a free ride any more, and there was no way I was going to stand up and say that they deserved to be treated with respect when they're charging £15 for a CD and had been shafting their artists and audiences senseless for decades.

Which made me realise this: the whole Variety Show thing, along with some of the more vitriolic press, simply confirmed that I didn't fit into the established classical world and I didn't fit into the crossover classical world. Instead I was shuffling along in my own little space, convinced I was doing something good and worthy, but having to accept that it was going to take a while to get onto solid ground and build things up.

Here too is the importance of good management. Denis is often more of a nurse/shrink/big brother than a manager. There are certain things I fear, and feel that were I to tweet them, talk about them in interviews or make them public, my career would probably dive-bomb into obscurity. There are things I cannot tell my lover, family, friends or even shrink. But Denis knows all of it. Our relationship is at the point, and has been for a long time, where I feel and act as if he is simply an extension of myself and so there's no need to hide anything – he is always there, always dependable, a given.

There is the professional stuff he does, which I guess is the main point of a manager. I look around at my piano world today and see a forthcoming series on Channel 4; concerts all around the world

from the Sydney Opera House to America, London to Barbados; a
live DVD; five albums; even my own line of shoes (shut up – they're
called Jimmy Shoes, at least until we get sued, and they are awesome;
designed by Tracey Neuls, a fan who wanted me to wear something
comfortable and high quality on stage, they don't disappoint, and will
be available online and in store by the time you read this); an income
that many music college graduates couldn't dream of earning; a royalty
percentage that is the highest I've ever heard of in the music sector;
and all of that is down to him. He scours contracts, hammers the
phone, pushes politely yet persistently in meetings, thinks of the bigger
picture all the time, has a plan and a vision and sticks to it no matter
what. He is a likeable Donald Trump in business and even more
talented in a world where I, left to my own devices, would do pretty
much anything for free simply because it involves getting to play music.

But then there is the stuff that keeps me alive, often smiling, able
to sleep calmly most nights. He has gone through a world of shit in
his lifetime. A hideous upbringing, violence, trauma, pain, heartache
and serious strife. And he has emerged whole, wise and with that
particular flavour of kindness and compassion that can only ever come
from shared pain. There are no office hours. It is a 24/7 relationship
where I can come to his house at 4 a.m. sobbing, share a cigarette
backstage before important gigs, send him a deluge of needy, worried
texts about money, concerts, reviews, girls, physical and mental health,
and know he will provide a moment of grace, of calmness and serenity
that will tide me over.

There is a reason that Lang Lang's people took my concert promoter
out for lunch and drilled her about what we were doing and how we

were doing it. Ditto why, just after *Razor Blades* came out, Michael Lang, the head of Deutsche Grammophon (once the most prestigious classical music label in the world) called Denis to tell us to hold off signing with anyone, get a bit more experience and then perhaps they might consider signing me up in a few months or a couple of years.

'Years?' Denis laughed. 'Michael, have you been reading the papers? Why would we wait for you that long – you probably won't have a job by next year.'

And if Michael had given us just one valid reason we might have considered it. But Denis knew, as did I, that the only way forward, the only realistic shot we had at reaching our goal, was to try doing things in a new way and avoid the established classical industry as much as possible.

It's funny, because fundamentally he and I are just two slightly deranged schmucks who seem to have found a really, really cool way to play and present the most incredible music ever written. And also lovely because when we met, Denis had no clue about classical music. Now he listens to it all of the time, treats the giant pieces I've introduced him to as his babies and has fallen in love with a whole new world. He is my target audience. Someone who kind of wants to know more about classical music, doesn't really know where to start, and doesn't want to hang around weirdos and old people to find out more about it.

Denis has got me into venues and situations I could never have even dreamt of. He and the team at GHP have got decent concert fees for some tattooed loser who wears jeans and swears too much and plays the piano perhaps as well as a bunch of music college undergraduates but certainly no better, and put their faith, money and energy into him, even when it looked like nothing would happen.

It feels harder in the UK sometimes, as there seems to be less desire to try things that at first glance seem inaccessible or requiring time and effort. But in 2011 I toured Australia and it really absolutely confirmed that there was something we were doing that could have an impact. We sold out two shows in Melbourne and had to add a third, I got on the news (for the right reason), played in Canberra, Sydney, Adelaide, Brisbane, got *Bullets and Lullabies* into the top twenty rock charts, consistently played to audiences aged in their early twenties who had never been to a piano recital before, and I spent a couple of weeks eating banana bread, having surprising massages (don't even ask what happens at the end over there) and noticing that there was a huge, welcoming response to classical music from people who would not have normally given two fucks.

Geoffrey Rush came to one of my Melbourne gigs. We shared a cigarette afterwards and I remember asking myself what the fuck I'd done to get to be this lucky. Especially because the day after I did a segment for ABC news with David Helfgott, whom Rush had played so brilliantly in the film *Shine*. Helfgott had listened to the live radio broadcast of one of the Melbourne concerts and loved it. He was, is, an amazing man. Troubled, manic, scary, brilliant and unique. And a great warning about where I could end up emotionally if I don't keep my shit together.

Denis had also been listening to the Melbourne gig back home in London where he had literally crawled back under the covers as he heard me cracking jokes about the Holocaust, AIDS and dwarf porn to a lovely Australian audience live on ABC radio. I blame the jet lag. And I love the Aussies even more for being so welcoming and open-hearted.

Once I got back, I realised perhaps Warner Bros wasn't the right way forward. Having failed to get the Royal Variety gig, there was no plan B and they kinda just gave up on me. I have huge respect for the guys there and they put so much time and effort in, but the fit wasn't quite right for the both of us. I had been signed to the world's largest rock label, but couldn't profit from it only because you can't make orange juice out of lemons no matter how much time and money you spend trying. If we had found a way to make it work I'd have stayed in a heartbeat, but somehow playing Beethoven when they were used to plugging and selling Green Day and Linkin Park was a stretch too far, no matter how noble or sincere the intentions. So we amicably parted ways.

I wanted to do a live album and went back to Signum for that. Steve Long, the boss at Signum, could not have been kinder or more supportive. We did two performances at a Brighton theatre that became album number four – 'Jimmy' (the name my friends call me).

What was lovely was that rather than simply having the music on the finished album, I wanted to keep all the introductions and chatting on there too. It was, in effect, an exact replica of the concert I did, complete with the odd wrong note, plenty of chatting, laughter, and, I hope, the unique energy of a live performance that is so hard to capture in a recording studio. God, that sounds pretentious. But you get the idea. With the talking included I believe it's a genuinely real, honest live album and, for classical at least, the first of its kind. And the fact that it is also the first classical album to have a 'parental advisory' sticker on it makes me, in a slightly puerile way, a little bit proud.

It was released at the very end of 2011, and 2012 and '13 were two of the biggest years of my life, both personally and professionally.

Schubert, Sonata No. 20, D959, Second Movement

Alexander Lonquich, Piano

(if you can find his recording anywhere.
Otherwise Severin von Eckardstein nails it
with appropriate madness)

In 1994, EMI released what was for me the greatest disc of Schubert's piano music ever made. A young pianist called Alexander Lonquich was at the keyboard. Born in Trier, Germany, but residing in Italy, Lonquich was EMI's shining star.

Bear in mind that this was a time when classical music had serious money. This was EMI in its heyday, with huge marketing spend and a loyal and large fan base. The main work on the CD was Schubert's immense A major Sonata, D959. As is the case with Beethoven, Schubert's last three sonatas (of which this is the second) are his crowning achievement. They are ethereal, mesmerising, astonishing and immortal. Schubert's madness has never been more clear in the bipolar slow movement where any pretence at tonality and structure flies out of the window, and the genius of the last movement of this piece is such that I can (and have) listened to it hundreds of times, not once being anything other than enraptured. It is, in my opinion, the greatest thing he ever wrote.

Hundreds of pianists have recorded this work, but Lonquich is in an entirely different league. He manages to do the impossible and make it seem that, even in its most insane moments, there is space between every note. The music floats into your ears and simply takes over your mind. I know it sounds pretentious and distinctly un-British, but I first listened to it after a piano lesson in Verona, sitting at a cafe in the sunshine, drinking the finest coffee known to man, and openly wept at the genius on display. It was a genuine reminder of everything that is great about the world.

Lonquich's sound, his staggering technique, his ability to make the entire sonata seep into every cell of your body and make you stare open-mouthed in wonderment is the rarest of feats. It is a disc I come back to again and again and again.

As an aside, because it's interesting to me, at a time of money, marketing, loyal fans and with the impressive weight of EMI behind him, according to a good friend and ex-flatmate of his who is also in the business, Lonquich's album, his superbly recorded, bar-raising reinvention of Schubert has, to date, sold just over seventy units. Seven zero.

THE THRILLS AND SPILLS OF 2012 began with Channel 4. They came to us via the production company that had done the Sky Arts series and suggested a one-off documentary looking at music and mental health. Which was perfect. All too often someone in my position is asked to front a programme for one of the major TV channels and ends up doing something that runs totally counter to their ideals and ideas. But they do it because, well, it's Channel 4, or the BBC or ITV or whatever. In this case I was lucky enough to find the perfect fit on my first shot. I'd done the Sky Arts series and the BBC4 documentary about Chopin so was used to filming, loved the whole process, and Denis and I had always dreamed of being on terrestrial TV. When I worked in the City, we used that awful phrase 'channel to market' all the time. And as far as classical was concerned, the biggest channel to market was terrestrial TV. It was the fastest and most effective way to get core classical music into people's lives and living rooms. It's what the major labels had always moaned about wanting because it was such a powerful medium, but could never seem to find the right people to do it.

We were due to start filming in July of 2012. The idea was for me to go into a secure, locked psychiatric ward (this time as a guest), meet some of their most vulnerable patients and talk about their histories, and then I was to find a piece of piano music I felt would resonate with them and play it just to them on a giant Steinway concert grand. It was, for me, a testament to the power of music and its ability to cut through even the heaviest medication and perhaps shine a little glimmer of light on an otherwise fucked situation.

Now I know that music heals. I know that it saved my life, kept me safe, gave me hope when there was none elsewhere. And the thought of capturing that, in some small way, on TV was an amazing opportunity for me. Alas a few days before filming started, my relationship fell apart, and this time it felt like it was for good.

It had been coming for a while. Both Hattie and I, despite sharing a seemingly bottomless pit of love, were on different pages. She wanted marriage and kids, I didn't feel brave enough to go down the road again after what had happened to me the first time. She had certain past traumas that had left her fragile in ways that made it hard for her to feel secure and confident, and I didn't make it any easier for her with my constant controlling and dickish behaviour. Ultimately we decided that we should end things, and in early June she moved out.

And the tragic thing is that the moment she did, I knew it was a huge mistake. Look, the easiest thing in the world is to cut and run. From anything, not just relationships. It neatly avoids taking responsibility for things, learning lessons that *have* to be learned at some point, reinforces blame and, in my case at least, ensured I would simply repeat the same shit with someone else.

I went off to the hospital, a couple of hours outside London, and started filming while she collected her things and emptied our flat. All of which meant I was stuck in a mental hospital, with a film crew, wanting to die, alone and afraid and miserable. Which made for good TV at the very least. I was there for a couple of weeks, meeting these astonishing patients, hearing stories that defied belief, many of which couldn't for legal reasons make the final edit. It had been very hard getting into the hospital in the first place – such is our culture that many of the staff thought we were an undercover *Panorama* crew or similar, ostensibly there to make a doc about the patients and music, but in reality there to expose their awful practices and show the world how dreadfully the patients were treated and how low the standard of care was.

Which was nuts, because the staff were, to a (wo)man, incredible. The patients had all been sectioned, had spent many, many years in hospital, many of them decades. They had violent backgrounds, severe self-harm issues, shatteringly awful histories and symptoms. And as the days went on I started to get more and more wobbly. The smells of the hospital, the medication times on the boards, the carpets, the air of desperation, sadness and everything else that comprises mental hospitals brought all of my stuff back, and the one person I wanted to call had moved out and moved on.

The crew were terrific, we did everything we needed to do, the patients were at once humbling and inspiring, and the time I spent there seemed to provide the director with enough material to make a 47-minute film.

I left and got the train back to London very late on a Sunday night. It was pissing with rain. I walked through my front door to an empty flat, Hattie's keys gently laid on the table, everything neat and tidy and soulless and quiet. I just sat there and cried, feeling very sorry for myself. And I felt that awful, creeping and all too familiar chill of destruction and depression knocking at the door.

Depression abhors a vacuum. Despite a run of concerts, filming, recording and writing, I suddenly found myself empty. There was very little in the diary, I was exhausted after the end of the relation-ship and an intense period of work on the documentary, alone in my flat, my son on the other side of the world, friends busy with their own lives. Denis was around, he always is, and yet when people like me spot a space we tend to tunnel into it rather than out of it. We're as stupid and as incapable of learning as moths circling a light bulb.

And the following twelve months were the closest I've been to disappearing for good since being hospitalised. The whole cosmic, self-help mantra of being given what you need when you need it, of needing to hit rock bottom, having to go through things rather than around them is, sadly, true. At least for me. If I'd weighed a few stone more, had the constitution to handle alcohol, heroin and crack, a lot of cash and no issue with sleeping with hookers, I could perhaps have got through things a different, slightly more entertaining way. But I finally had time, space and loneliness forced upon me by some force greater than myself and, as it turned out, I came through the other side ready, for the first time in my life, to live well.

There are not seven stages of grief. Not in my experience. Why does everything have to be boiled down into bite-sized, manageable, understandable chunks? Are we that fucking stupid and incapable of living without definitives or corners or edges? There was just one long stage of hell. It would switch in an instant from absolute anger to inconsolable sadness to despair, hopelessness, an unfillable emptiness. There were occasional moments of peace, usually as a result of having only two hours' sleep and being too tired to feel anything. There was the occasional relapse into self harm and cutting, a couple of disastrous dates, one brief, mental fling and a soulless one-night stand, but primarily there was an awful lot of time on my own, thinking, sitting, feeling. Without medication. It was a first for me, and something that was inevitable, essential and, more by dumb luck than anything else, ultimately redemptive and restorative.

There was a certain desolate routine that I stumbled into. Up at three or four in the morning after a few hours' sleep, giant pot of coffee, couple of hours of piano in my little spare bedroom, more coffee, endless cigarettes, talk radio for company, more piano, shuffling out to Starbucks when it opened and watching, with open hostility, those couples going to work holding hands. Glazed eyes, 'fuck off' tattooed invisibly on my forehead, losing weight day by day. There was no focus in my life other than on its lack of focus. And that is a terrifying thing for someone who has entertained thoughts of suicide or self-harm. And the most painful thing was not that I had lost the one true love of my life, but that she was, in my head as per usual, going about her life with a spring in her step, having spectacular sex with a succession of handsome, well-built, rich men, partying until the small hours and giggling with joy the whole time.

I know there's nothing new here. Nothing that isn't happening to a million unfortunate bastards every fucking day. And yet when it's happening we all feel like we are the only ones. Grief and sadness is always wretchedly unique.

Denis and various friends tried their hardest to help but I guess I didn't want to be helped. It became apparent that this was not simply pain that came from the break-up of a relationship. It was bigger than that. Evidently, after a few weeks, most people would simply snap out of it, move on to someone new, put it down to life experience. Hattie and I had had five years, which was long, but by no means seriously long-term. We hadn't had children, hadn't been married, had only lived together for a couple of years. But I simply could not get over it. If anything, the pain was getting worse.

Six months down the line I was still in pieces. Everything I saw reminded me of her, everything I did was empty because she wasn't there. Even now I hate myself slightly for just how full of self-pity I seemed. I was a friend's worst nightmare. The crushing bore, obsessed with his own pain, with no room for any other news.

Nothing was working, and it felt time-sensitive. Like chances are I would not make it if things carried on much longer. I made a new will, wrote goodbye notes to a select few, played around with the idea of ending things once and for all. And once again, Jack stopped me from doing it just by existing. I made a goodbye video for him, watched it back and knew then and there that it wasn't a viable solution. I could not, just absolutely could not leave him. It didn't matter that we saw each other only a few times a year.

I did the occasional concert on autopilot (grim, jet-lagged performances in Chicago, Hong Kong, a few in London), practised every day, did what I could to function at the bare minimum.

What was lovely was how, despite my mood, despite giving concerts where some were good enough and some were, to my mind, a bit shabby, my audiences were consistently, overwhelmingly supportive and brilliant. For all my personal ups and downs and raging, self-critical head, they were so incredibly kind and reassuring.

One highlight was when I flew to Austria to play two concerts in one day. We landed and drove to the British ambassador's residence where I played for ninety minutes to an assorted audience of well-heeled Viennese and English socialites and influencers (whatever the fuck that means). And then immediately afterwards I was driven to the Konzerthaus for an evening recital – a concert hall steeped in tradition and history and Austria's equivalent to the Wigmore Hall.

Backstage they had a fridge full of chocolate, a Nespresso machine, bananas and Haribo (Southbank Centre take note). And even more delightfully, a smoking room where I sat with my coffee and chatted to a few violinists and cellists – who turned out to be members of the Vienna Philharmonic. Feeling a little like a football fan in the Stamford Bridge players' cafeteria, I dribbled and blushed my way through five minutes of music chat (turns out Sakari Oramo is a proper gent) before rushing back to the piano, realising stupidly late that I was about to play Beethoven, Schubert and Chopin to a sold-out Konzerthaus in bloody Vienna.

And it went well. Good enough, anyway. Which is the best I can hope for. Five encores and the terrific realisation that the Viennese have a sense of humour even about what they hold most sacred – comparing Franck Ribéry to Schubert (short, aesthetically challenged, genius) was met with genuine laughter, and not just from my mum, who had made the trip and doesn't even know who Franck Ribéry is.

I will always be stupidly grateful to this hall full of strangers whose kindness and support and applause made life a little more colourful and a little less threatening.

It started to go from grim to dangerous on New Year's Eve. Never, ever scour Facebook looking for evidence that your ex is having a better time now she is without you. Ever. Turned out that Hattie's New Year's Eve was everything it should be for a hot young single girl in London. Guys, parties, dancing, short skirts, more parties, more (ripped, handsome, cuntish) guys. Turns out that perhaps my toxic imagination wasn't so far-fetched after all. Me, I was in bed alone by 9.30 p.m. desperate to escape into sleep. Something snapped.

At 6 a.m. I still hadn't slept and called Denis. He answered (he always does) and I went round to his place and just sobbed at his kitchen table. I know that I am in my mid to late thirties. I know that my emotional reaction to all of this is that of a seven-year-old boy. But I am incapable of shifting it, working through it, beating it. And if I surrender to it I believe I will die.

And then Denis gave me a couple of books and suggested I read them.

He said to me:

'James I need to tell you that I've made my peace with you not making it. I am ready to get the call telling me you've been found dead, and much though it hurts, I am prepared for it. You do what you need to do, but please know it's in your hands now.'

And that was a big enough shock for me to get off my ass, if only a tiny bit, and start reading. I didn't want to, I fought against it, but it was just so clear that I had to if I wanted to stay alive.

This is becoming a difficult thing to write about. How easy it is to put on paper the negative things, the rapes, trauma, divorce, self-harming. How difficult to write about good things and solutions for fear of sounding like a dope-smoking, tofu-eating, dreadlocked hippie. The two books I was given that day were about the body and mind's response to trauma (*Waking the Tiger*) and the inner child (*Homecoming*). I know. Pass the bucket.

In the most British of ways I am mortified at having to acknowledge that I had to go so far down the hole that I needed books like this to survive. Spending time in a mental hospital is somehow like having a giant scar that at least garners a certain amount of respect. Self-help books? Like I said, mortifying.

The thing is they didn't only help me survive, they did something much, much greater than that. They took the beginning I had made in hospital in Phoenix and helped to nurture and grow that into a deep and long-lasting foundation upon which the rest of my life could be built – reliably, gently and solidly. Those books got past that odd kink in my character that will allow me to give time, money, effort and energy to someone else who is in pain but will resolutely balk at the idea of doing those things for myself. I had finally run out of options and started to honestly appraise things and start mending them.

Clearly I wasn't going to be capable of any kind of relationship, with the emotional and physiological responses of a child. I was intrinsically damaged, selfish, egocentric and self-involved, and the only way out of that was to go back, experience all of it again as an adult and try and mend things. And that's what I did. For several weeks I meditated every day, often twice a day. I read the books, did the exercises suggested, wrote, even prayed, sat with the feelings without distraction and went into myself as I'd never done before.

The most helpful thing I learned was to experience painful, shameful feelings but to drop any kind of storyline attached to them. In the past I'd feel shame or disgust or self-hatred, and as I felt those things I'd narrate them in my head, give them pictures and words, explore the reasons behind them, indulge in nurturing, judging and growing the feelings even more. Now I learned, slowly, to simply sit and notice them with curiosity, no labels, stories or judgment. I would just see where in the body they were gathered (invariably the heart or stomach), watch them, experience the pain, sit with it. And I promise you, when you do that, it all starts to heal. Slowly but surely it starts to heal and soften and lessen.

And before long, something wonderful happened – I somehow made a connection with the me that existed before that gym teacher got his filthy hands on me, I realised that I wasn't bad or toxic, I started to allow myself to mend and forgive myself and accept things for the first time.

Amazing, isn't it? That big a statement in one sentence. As if I'd undergone decades of trauma, personal reflection, medication, therapy, struggle and analysis and then suddenly something popped and I became whole again. *Again*. Not for the first time. But whole like I was when I was three years old and really fucking happy.

And everything changed. Music became even more alive and important. Sleep started to become natural and restorative. My guts stopped exploding five times a day. My various squeaks, tics and twitches, which had come back, eased up. I didn't have to flick light switches and tap out specific rhythms every few hours to prevent bad things from happening. I actually forgave myself for something that no one in their right mind would see as my transgression but that I had felt, since the age of five, was my fault.

And although there had been several false starts over the years – shrinks, hospitals, twelve-step meetings, medication, psychiatrists, workshops, a plethora of mental health remedies – it was, in addition to months of work in Phoenix, these two books, given to me by my manager on a rainy, miserable New Year's Day, that finally brought about my new beginning.

We are riddled with trauma. Abandonment, divorce, violence, abuse of every kind, neglect, alcoholism, anger, blame, judgment, religion, bullying – a thousand different forms of hell surround us from our first days on this planet. Sometimes intentionally, often totally unconsciously, we are, I believe, the walking wounded from a very young age. Some people seem to adjust well despite it, some don't. And although I tried everything I could to distract from that hurt, I could not outrun it.

And while forgiveness and meditation, reading and writing, talking and sharing all help, creativity is, for me, one of the most profound ways through trauma. Even more so when all that New-Age, tree-hugging stuff has finally cleared enough space in my head to allow me to be free enough to explore creativity in a new and slightly more manageable way.

Three months into this new chapter in my life, I had never been so in love with the piano, with playing, writing, reading, devouring anything and everything creative. And I wrote an article for the

Guardian that seemed to resonate. It was shared over 100,000 times, I got emails telling me it was read out in school assemblies in Texas and offices in Australia, hundreds of messages letting me know how much it had helped people move through into new areas of wonder. I wrote it at 6 a.m. one morning and it felt like the closest thing I've ever got to a mission statement.

Here it is:

'Find what you love and let it kill you'
Guardian Culture Blog, 26 April 2013

After the inevitable 'How many hours a day do you practise?' and 'Show me your hands', the most common thing people say to me when they hear I'm a pianist is 'I used to play the piano as a kid. I really regret giving it up.' I imagine authors have lost count of the number of people who have told them they 'always had a book inside them'. We seem to have evolved into a society of mourned and misplaced creativity. A world where people have simply surrendered to (or been beaten into submission by) the sleepwalk of work, domesticity, mortgage repayments, junk food, junk TV, junk everything, angry ex-wives, ADHD kids and the lure of eating chicken from a bucket while emailing clients at 8 p.m. on a weekend.

Do the maths. We can function — sometimes quite brilliantly — on six hours' sleep a night. Eight hours of work was more than good enough for centuries (oh the desperate irony that we actually work longer hours since the invention of the internet and smartphones).

Four hours will amply cover picking the kids up, cleaning the flat, eating, washing and the various etceteras. We are left with six hours. 360 minutes to do whatever we want. Is what we want simply to numb out and give Simon Cowell even more money? To scroll through Twitter and Facebook looking for romance, bromance, cats, weather reports, obituaries and gossip? To get nostalgically, painfully drunk in a pub where you can't even smoke?

What if you could know everything there is to know about playing the piano in under an hour (something the late, great Glenn Gould claimed, correctly I believe, was true)? The basics of how to practise and how to read music, the physical mechanics of finger movement and posture, all the tools necessary to actually play a piece – these can be written down and imparted like a flat-pack furniture how-to-build-it manual; it then is down to you to scream and howl and hammer nails through fingers in the hope of deciphering something unutterably alien until, if you're very lucky, you end up with something halfway resembling the end product.

What if for a couple of hundred quid you could get an old upright on eBay delivered? And then you were told that with the right teacher and 40 minutes' proper practice a day you could learn a piece you've always wanted to play within a few short weeks. Is that not worth exploring?

What if rather than a book club you joined a writer's club? Where every week you had to (really had to) bring three pages of your novel, novella, screenplay and read them aloud?

What if, rather than paying £70 a month for a gym

membership that delights in making you feel fat, guilty and a world away from the man your wife married, you bought a few blank canvases and some paints and spent time each day painting your version of 'I love you' until you realised that any woman worth keeping would jump you then and there just for that, despite your lack of a six-pack?

I didn't play the piano for 10 years. A decade of slow death by greed working in the City, chasing something that never existed in the first place (security, self-worth, Don Draper albeit a few inches shorter and a few women fewer). And only when the pain of not doing it got greater than the imagined pain of doing it did I somehow find the balls to pursue what I really wanted and had been obsessed by since the age of seven – to be a concert pianist.

Admittedly I went a little extreme – no income for five years, six hours a day of intense practice, monthly four-day long lessons with a brilliant and psychopathic teacher in Verona, a hunger for something that was so necessary it cost me my marriage, nine months in a mental hospital, most of my dignity and about 35lbs in weight. And the pot of gold at the end of the rainbow is not perhaps the happy ending I'd envisaged as I lay in bed aged 10 listening to Horowitz devouring Rachmaninov at Carnegie Hall.

My life involves endless hours of repetitive and frustrating practising, lonely hotel rooms, dodgy pianos, aggressively bitchy reviews, isolation, confusing airline reward programmes, physiotherapy, stretches of nervous boredom (counting ceiling tiles backstage as the house slowly fills up) punctuated by short moments of extreme pressure (playing 120,000 notes from memory in the right order with the right fingers, the right sound, the right pedalling while chatting about the composers and pieces and knowing there are critics, recording devices, my mum, the ghosts of the past, all there watching), and perhaps most crushingly, the realisation that I will never, ever give the perfect recital. It can only ever, with luck, hard work and a hefty dose of self-forgiveness, be 'good enough'.

And yet. The indescribable reward of taking a bunch of ink on paper from the shelf at Chappell of Bond Street. Tubing it home, setting the score, pencil, coffee and ashtray on the piano and emerging a few days, weeks or months later able to perform something that some mad, genius, lunatic of a composer 300 years ago heard in his head while out of his mind with grief or love or syphilis. A piece of music that will always baffle the greatest minds in the world, that simply cannot be made sense of, that is still living and floating in the ether and will do so for yet more centuries to come. That is extraordinary. And I did that. I do it, to my continual astonishment, all the time.

The government is cutting music programmes in schools and slashing arts grants as gleefully as a morbidly American kid in Baskin Robbins. So if only to stick it to the man, isn't it worth fighting back in some small way? So write your damn book. Learn a Chopin prelude, get all Jackson Pollock with the kids, spend a few hours writing a haiku. Do it because it counts even without the fanfare, the money, the fame and Heat photo-shoots that all our children now think they're entitled to because Harry Styles has done it.

Charles Bukowski, hero of angsty teenagers the world over, instructs

us to 'find what you love and let it kill you'. Suicide by creativity
is something perhaps to aspire to in an age where more people know
Katie Price better than the 'Emperor Concerto'.

The response to this piece made me realise that there is a way of doing things that has an impact. That we can all be a little less separate and a little more together. When I got asked to write this book I suggested on Twitter that people join me and that we all write a thousand words a day. And knowing that in a couple of months there will be a bunch of new novels, plays, novellas, short stories out there, that a bunch of us are doing something small and yet giant every day, is special to me.

It all ties in with what I do every day. Learning a new piece involves the same process. Manageable chunks of time, focus, discipline, honest work. I decide what piece I'm going to learn, head down to the music store, come home with a score, put coffee, an ashtray, a pencil and a metronome on top of the piano and start with the first page. I go through page by page, line by line, figuring out the best fingering to use. I break the difficult technical bits down into chunks and use little practising tricks to learn them. I repeat and repeat, consciously aware of every single note and, over time, over an hour or two or four each day, it builds until I'm walking out on stage a few weeks later and playing it from memory. This is what life is for me. It is exhilarating, inspiring, rewarding and dignified. It applies not just to music and writing but to relationships, love, friendship, care. It is, ultimately, about how we express ourselves and how we value ourselves. And in my small little world, it feels like a revolution. It allows me to replace all

of the heavy, negative, bullshit energy in my life with something liber-
ating and valuable. It gives me permission to stop being a victim and
contribute something deeper to my world. It is, fundamentally, a
transference of negative energy to positive. It is something that can
grow by attraction rather than promotion because it works. It needs
no hard sell. No sell of any kind. And, miraculously and joyfully, I am
living it.

Beethoven, Piano Concerto No. 5 ('Emperor'), Second Movement
Radu Lupu, Piano

There's a piece of music I'd like played at my funeral. Properly played – live, with orchestra and a decent pianist, not pumped out of speakers in the drizzle as people loaf around thinking about snacks.

It's one of the first pieces of music I cried to. Beethoven wrote five piano concertos and the last one is titled the 'Emperor' because it's typically bombastic, heroic and in your face. (Much like Napoleon was, despite being so ickle.) The two outer movements are exhilarating – deluges of notes, cascades of fireworks, electrifying and tumultuous thrills and spills. And they flank a middle movement of breathtaking beauty and serenity. It was all a bit much for my younger mind to handle, but now as an adult it simply demonstrates everything that music is and does.

Fucking Beethoven . . .

I HAVE ALWAYS FELT THAT the most profound problem with my industry is that it takes the focus off creativity and places it instead on ego. Classical music has become about appearance (sacred or sacrilegious, take your pick), money-making, dressing up, pomp and prestige, rather than simply being of service to the music. And it's not just the musicians who are complicit but the surrounding industry too. The classical music awards ceremonies are rife with it. Dire, evil, despicable horrors that have nothing to do with music at all.

The Classic BRIT Awards represent the epitome of what is so dreadfully wrong with the classical music industry. In 2012 I couldn't hold back any longer and wrote a piece for the *Telegraph* about just how monstrous they, and the people running it, were. The full text is in the Appendix of this book, but the short version is as follows: if you are curious about classical music you would be better educated, better served, and better off spending thirty minutes watching Leonard Bernstein talk about Beethoven on YouTube than sitting through that stinking, three-hour fuckathon.

Ironically, for many years I thought the Gramophone Awards (more serious, more glamorous, with bona fide classical musicians winning awards) were the real deal. Until I went to them for the first time expecting a bit of that glamour and depth. It was a huge mistake, and one I found particularly crushing – even these guys, the so-called 'proper' end of classical music, were so far up their own asses they could barely breath. This time I wrote about them for the *Guardian* (again, reprinted in the Appendix) and called it how I saw it. They had the editor of *Gramophone* write a response on why I'd missed the point, but I remain convinced I didn't. These guys are totally responsible for the very things they are complaining about.

When I wrote about this stuff in the papers I got so many supportive and lovely messages, especially from people in the industry who simply couldn't lend their support publicly and stay employed. Much of the feedback in the comments threads asked for solutions. Quite rightly – it is easy to piss and moan, much harder to offer workable solutions that can bring about change. Only it isn't hard at all.

My solution? Fuck the lot of them. Play what you want, where you want, how you want and to whom you want. Do it naked, do it wearing jeans, doing it while cross-dressing. Do it at midnight or 3 p.m. Do it in bars and pubs, halls and theatres. Do it for free. Do it for charity. Do it in schools. Make it inclusive, accessible, respectful, authentic. Give it back to whom it belongs. Don't let a few geriatric, inbred morons dictate how this immortal, incredibly wonderful, God-given music should be presented. We're bigger than that. God knows, the music is too.

There are thousands of students at music college who would love the experience of playing to an audience that doesn't simply comprise other music students, and if they don't love or want that experience, they're not going to last long. Do it for travel expenses in local schools, halls, clubs and think of it as a warm-up for paid gigs. I would (and do) happily perform a few times a year for free at a school or hospital – it helps me prepare for professional engagements, allows me to share something I love, and is hugely useful in building up repertoire and stamina. Get in touch and ask if that's something you'd like me to do for you.

Alongside the typical 7.30/8 p.m. recitals, give concerts at 6.30 p.m. for an hour so people can come straight from work and listen and still be out in time for a meal with a hot date or to get home in time to put the kids to bed. Or perform at 10 p.m. when people have had a chance to go out for dinner beforehand and want to finish off the evening with some music.

Give music away for free. Not whole albums, necessarily, but tracks. Put them up on SoundCloud and allow downloads. Send them via email to a fan list, however small. Get the music out there in the public domain where it belongs rather than in sweaty practice rooms or buried under a million other albums on Amazon.

Play different venues, from traditional classical ones to clubs. Limelight at the 100 Club, Classical Revolution, the Yellow Lounge and a host of others are all putting on classical music nights. And, if you want to reach a new audience rather than an established one, then when you play don't programme overly long, terrifically complex contemporary shit to show how avant-garde you are. If that's your thing then play fifteen minutes of it alongside Brahms and Chopin because, well, they're Brahms and Chopin and no matter how genuine your love of Stockhausen and Birtwistle, we both know there's no real competition there.

Share concerts between artists like Beethoven did. Have some chamber music, some solo music, some songs. Variety is always good.

Let the audience bring drinks in, engage with them, chat to them both from the stage and on social media. This is a huge point. Recently I was hanging with the boss of one of the major labels over lunch and discussing how they could sell more records. He was telling me how most of their artists are incredibly difficult – they refuse to play certain venues that aren't deemed prestigious enough, don't want to do interviews, don't feel comfortable engaging with audiences. Which is fine until you realise that gone are the days of simply relying on the record labels to drum up business and sell albums and tickets. We musicians need to engage and form a relationship with our audience that goes beyond the few autograph hunters post-gig. Be approachable, respond to tweets and Facebook messages, crack jokes, be human, drop the whole 'artist shrouded in his own genius' bullshit. Because if you don't or cannot do that, unless you are a one-in-a-generation talent, you're going to struggle. It is no longer enough to simply excel at making music. Make sure your management and label are on the same page too.

And if they're not then change them. I've been incredibly lucky with my manager. And also with my label, Signum, whose boss Steve continues to be an absolute Don. And yet there is more that I want to do. I am so eager to break away from the self-dug trench that classical music is in that I am in the process of setting up my own record label, Instrumental Records. I want to put together my very own creative hub.

What if the majority of female classical musicians weren't marketed on what they looked like? If there was simply no need to record versions of *Les Mis* for cello and piano in order to flog albums? If labels didn't tell you what to record, choose the album cover photos, get some old-school academic to write the liner notes, try impotently to plug it to their 1,000 Twitter followers, get it on to Amazon for £14 more than a month after its release date?

Instrumental is a label where I can give the musicians the opportunity to record what they want. We will design beautiful albums, tour as a label, doing concerts that respect the music, musicians and audience, foster new talent regardless of age and looks, pay musicians the royalties they deserve, give them better all-round control of what they want to do, and encourage and nurture a following on and offline that feeds into the whole musical revolution we are a part of.

We could put on an awards ceremony that really does celebrate the best that classical music has to offer – not cheap, dumbed-down shit and not back-slapping, self-congratulatory wank. Just brilliant musicians, warm, amenable hosts, laughter, music, inspiration and delight in a sector of the arts that has always aimed either too high or too low and been terrified of everything in between.

And the best part about it is that it looks as though I will have the implicit support of one of the country's most powerful TV broadcasters because of the work I'm doing with Channel 4. In many ways, Savile aside, I love and admire the BBC. But they seem to be preaching to the converted; their classical music shows, such as they are, don't look to try to attract new audiences but seem content with the existing ones. With the backing of Channel 4 and by creating my own label, artist and audience will be on the same page, the music will come first and I will finally have a chance to work towards the dream I've had ever since I can remember.

And if you're reading this and have something to say then come and join me. Whether you're with one of the big labels and bored of being treated like shit, or you've never recorded before but are hungry to do so, let me know. If you are horrified that rather than finding another, shorter piece, Lang Lang happily cut out over half of a Chopin polonaise at the Classic BRITs without explaining why simply because it was going to be on TV and had to fit under the magical three-minute ADHD concentration limit, if you're willing and able to talk to your audience, to spread something pure and lovely, to say 'fuck you' to the 20 per cent of audience members who'd prefer you to shut up and simply play the notes, then let's make albums, let's tour, let's do something magnificent and brilliant and worthwhile and of service to the music, the audience and the performer.

I did an evening at the Barbican with Stephen Fry talking about the issues facing classical music. I played and took questions and we debated. We charged £5, it was rammed, and there was a genuine hunger for music, discussion and performance. Imagine touring a group of incredibly talented musicians who can and will take part in Q&As with their audiences, who will engage them and introduce pieces, who will give free master-classes and talks, share their opinions honestly, do what they can to further musical education in this country.

OK, I know it sounds a little like some utopian vision of mine that occurred while taking a really long dump, but trust me, I will make this happen.

I went recently to a middle school in leafy Hertfordshire. It was a pre-production trip for a new Channel 4 series. I wanted to see what the state of affairs is concerning music tuition in schools. I was confronted with a class of thirty children who were engaged, eager, passionate and genuinely keen to immerse themselves in music. Their (brilliant) teacher has a total annual budget of £400 for 160 children.

Necessity being the motherfucker of invention, what I witnessed was a kind of miniature *Stomp* – dustbins, margarine tins and chocolate boxes used as instruments, a cello that looked as if it had been used as firewood, and a couple of mangled trumpets that were unplayable. There is something hideously wrong with an education system that has all the necessary ingredients for learning – passion, curiosity, incredibly hard-working and inventive teachers – and rewards that with mops and dustbins rather than instruments and subsidies for private tuition.

How many future Adeles, Ashkenazys, Rattles or Elton Johns are we missing out on simply because they haven't been given the opportunity to explore music-making? Perhaps more importantly, regardless of future commercial success, how many young creative minds are the government stifling out of laziness, vote-chasing and misplaced priorities? Another one of the arts is biting the dust. In the age of entitlement and instant fame that is so encouraged and idealised by *Heat* magazine and its ilk, at a time where record companies won't give you a second glance unless you've got 20,000 Twitter followers, a million YouTube hits and an album already written and produced, someone felt it a worthy idea to treat music education as an extravagance rather than a basic right. If that doesn't change, the impact cannot fail to be far-reaching and long-lasting. And so let's change it.

Look at what Sir Nick Serota has done with the Tate – once the privilege of a tiny minority, now over 7,000,000 visitors a year come and explore a world that would have been totally alien to most a couple of decades ago. He and his team have somehow loosened the stranglehold on the culture of modern art and flung open its doors to everyone, and they haven't had to change or dumb down the art works themselves in order to do it. Why not do the same with classical music but without using gimmicks, shit crossover music and boobs to achieve it? In many ways, classical music is the last art form to be opened up to one and all. And, fuck me, it is long overdue. Even more shamefully, it is not just because of the labels, the industry as a whole and the managers that we are in this situation, but also very much because of the artists and musicians themselves.

Classical music has apparently needed saving for a long time now. The demise of the industry has been predicted for over a decade and there are repeated cries for an urgent overhaul, together with the obligatory panicked squawks for drastic change in promotion, branding and presentation.

I agree that something needs to change. Not to 'save the industry'. Not to continue to ensure conductors can get paid £50,000 for a night's work. Not even to ensure that London's plethora of world-famous orchestras can continue to survive (although I desperately hope they do). I simply cannot make my peace with the fact that so few people are offered it as a valid choice.

The Proms has been heading in the right direction for a long time and is something we should be immensely proud of. When it opened its booking lines this year, it sold over 80,000 tickets in the first few hours. We should be proud to host the largest music festival in the world, attracting the brightest and best talent there is. The concerts are broadcast on radio, online and often on TV. The music reaches millions. What do the Proms do right to beat all the odds when everywhere else there are complaints about dwindling audiences? Is it perhaps the fact that no one gives a fuck what you wear as an audience member? The variety of the programming? Start times that include lunchtime, early evening, evening and late night?

No doubt all of the above. But for me, the overriding reason for the success of the Proms has got to be the fact that it doesn't have its head up its arse. It doesn't speak down to the public; it simply manages to give the impression that whatever your knowledge of classical music, whatever your experience, your likes, dislikes, dress sense, background or intelligence, you are very, very welcome. If you want to clap between movements, then knock yourself out. Don't know how to pronounce the name of the composer? Who cares? Don't feel the urge to announce loudly and smugly the name of the encore the soloist has decided to play? Even better. And it does this in a way that few, if any, of the other big halls manage to do.

The Proms also, of course, flies the flag for the obscene amount of talent our country has to offer – Stephen Hough, Paul Lewis, Nicola Benedetti, Benjamin Grosvenor etc all feature prominently. And if somehow we can translate this idea from the Proms to classical music as a whole in the UK, then the future will look very rosy indeed. It is starting to happen already – more people in the US went to a classical concert last year than to a football game. But we must not allow the momentum to fade away.

Rachmaninov, 'Rhapsody on a Theme of Paganini'

Zoltán Kocsis, Piano

Sergei Rachmaninov. A composer I love so much that I've had his name tattooed in Cyrillic into my forearm. A giant, 6 foot 6, manic, miserable, bipolar, millionaire virtuoso pianist and composer. At a time when Stravinsky, Schoenberg and others were railing against the 'tyranny of the bar line' and celebrating the 'emancipation of the dissonance' by pushing the boundaries of tonality beyond breaking point, Sergei stood firm, Romantic machine guns blazing away, and pumped out piece after piece of extraordinary depth, poetry and brilliance.

He was a chain smoker, underwent hypnosis to help conquer his depression, married his first cousin, and had such monumentally large hands that he could span twelve piano keys with one hand.

So many composers have written pieces based on Paganini's famous theme – from Brahms to Liszt to Lutoslawski. Rachmaninov's is the daddy of them all. All the more so given it was written by a guy once referred to as a 'six-foot scowl'.

IN MARCH 2013, AFTER NINE months apart, Hattie and I started, very slowly, to talk about things. I was aware how much I needed to prove to her that I was not the terrified, flighty, control freak I had been for the five years we had been together previously. I still am aware of that. And she was aware that she missed me like crazy and had only really met freaks and weirdos, despite the allure and freedom of the single life. And after a few months of giving, listening, genuinely trying to be the best version of myself despite frequently falling short, I met her in the secret garden in Regent's Park and asked her to marry me.

She said yes.

She may change her mind. She may decide it ain't for her. There are any number of reasons it may not work out. But I know, absolutely, categorically, for the first time, that I am giving it my best shot and will continue to do so for as long as she'll have me.

It had taken me five years of being with Hattie to figure out what was going on, what I was doing wrong and, more importantly, the solution to it.

There are so many self-help books about love and relationships. They use words like 'co-dependency', 'boundaries' and 'mirroring'. They're brilliant to read but they have rarely worked for me. In my opinion they are similar to those *Men's Health/Cosmopolitan* cover stories about perfect abs – worthy and exciting for about four minutes until you realise it involves a total 180-degree change in diet, exercise, discipline and routine. It's hysterical that I'm about to offer relationship advice. But hear this – ask a guy who's used heroin for years and then stopped how he did it and it'll be a hell of a lot more informative than some GP who wouldn't even know how to shoot up properly.

I've had a train-wreck of a marriage and almost lost the one great love of my life because I was trying to figure out how to do this shit on my own. And finally, although it's taken me fifteen years, I've managed to figure out a relationship guide that seems to work for me. If you can get rid of your ego, it's simple. If you can't, it'll never work. But the one thing that is abundantly clear is that the problem is you and never the other person.

Argue all you want about why I'm wrong about that, I couldn't give less of a fuck. I guarantee you that if there is something 'wrong' in your relationship, if you are unhappy and starting any sentence with 'if only he/she did/didn't . . .' then you're fucked, the relationship will not last and you'll be miserable. Which is fine for some people, especially people like me, because I loved feeling miserable. It gave me energy, reinforced my beliefs that the whole world was both shit and actively against me, and kept me nice and comfortable in my little self-pitying huddle.

It amazes me how many people love being unhappy. Unhappy about their bodies, sex lives, relationships, jobs, careers, families, homes, holidays, haircuts whatever. Our whole cultural identity is centred around not being good enough, constantly needing things that are shinier, faster, smaller, bigger, better. The advertising industry makes a fortune from it, the pharmaceutical, tobacco and alcohol industries also clean up as a result. People used to be happier. Much, much happier. Society during times of rationing, immense economic hardship and war was emotionally better-off, more closely knit and fulfilled than we are today with our fucking iPhones and fibre-optic broadband packages.

And we transfer all of those expectations onto our lovers. After the initial phase of mind-altering chemicals wears off (six months if you're lucky, usually a few weeks), men want women who are younger, tighter, filthier, hotter, sexier and skinnier. Women want more security – men who are richer, more emotional, stronger, empathic, talkative and confident. It's bullshit, but it is woven into the very fabric of our society. If, at this moment, you are with someone you love and you both want to settle down then there are a few simple things to be done that will pretty much guarantee you a happy, long-lasting relationship.

First off, you're wrong. It doesn't matter about what; if you know you're right, if all your friends tell you you're right, you're wrong. He forgot your anniversary and you're angry? You're wrong to be angry. Shut up. She keeps moaning about how much time you spend focused on work and nags you over and over again about it and you're pissed at her because of it? You're wrong. Stop being a dick. The biggest killer in any relationship is point-scoring. The great Persian poet, Rumi, wrote, 'somewhere out there, beyond ideas of right and wrong, there is a garden. I'll meet you there.' I have a pal who'd gone to couples therapy with his girlfriend and used to save up shit to ambush her with in their session. One week they'd been given homework to do and she hadn't done it. Clean forgot. He'd done his of course. Did he gently remind her about it, hoping that if they both did it the chances were good they could move forward and get closer together? Did he fuck. He delighted in the fact she hadn't, waited until they were in the session and then pounced like some smug fucking kid who'd finally done something right in class and wanted the whole world to know about it. Jesus.

Celebrate being wrong. Come from a position of 'I have got to work so fucking hard to make up for being wrong all the time in the hope she'll forgive me' and you'll be golden. Treat every meal/outing/walk/talk together as a first date with someone you are desperate to impress. Worry about what to wear, get anxious about whether or not you'll get something in your teeth over dinner, wash your ball sack thoroughly on the off chance you'll get lucky, bring flowers, ask for the most romantic table in the restaurant, be present and listen to every word spoken as if your life depended on it.

Give. Give all of the time. Give until you are exhausted and then give some more. When she's driving you nuts and you just want to throw yourself out of the window, go and make her a cup of tea, give her a massage, go down on her, buy her a fucking diamond. It is the most amazing exercise. Do it for a month and see what a difference it makes. And don't you fucking dare do it with any expectation of rewards or thanks. Do it because you love this person, they are spectacular, you adore them and you want them. If these things weren't true you wouldn't be together. Do it because deep down you know that you should be so fucking lucky to have the opportunity to go out in the freezing cold and driving rain to buy her her favourite kind of flowers.

Take a vow that – barring infidelity or serious abuse – leaving is off the table. It is not even to be discussed. The starting point is you are together, a team, full stop, end of. Any problems, no matter how serious, are dealt with as a team. There is simply no walking away. And take that vow in the same way as smokers who have successfully quit have taken the same vow about cigarettes. No matter what, they do not light up. Doing the same thing with marriage/relationships is ten times easier because cigarettes won't blow you and they'll eventually kill you. You're simply committing to be with this person no matter what, to stand together, to fight alongside each other, to be a united front, to be bigger than the sum of your parts. It's what you told her hundreds of times in the early days, what you've written to her thousands of times every time you texted you loved her, what you whispered in her ear every time you fucked. Man up, stick to your word, own it.

Do not ask questions about each other's pasts. Under no circumstances ask about exes, how many lovers they had, did they ever do anal with anyone, did they used to swallow, have you been to this country/hotel/restaurant with anyone else etc etc. Do not analyse the relationship with one another, do not examine where you are or where you're going. There is no possible upside to doing so.

Anticipate the other person's needs, do things that make them feel good, even if you think it's stupid, wrong, indulgent. Take ten minutes at the end of each day to check in with each other. Five minutes for each person to chat uninterrupted about their day – a few things they're grateful for, a few things the other one has done that touched them, a few things they're excited about, a few things they're worried about. Always end with an 'I love you' and a kiss. Always.

This is all especially important if you have kids. Your kids should know absolutely, and beyond question, that Mum/Dad comes first. You guys are the primary relationship and deserve the main focus. Love your kids, spoil them rotten, be there for them and give them everything you didn't get from your parents. But never, ever cut short a conversation with your wife just because they come barrelling into the room demanding a fucking ice cream. Don't change your plans to indulge them. Don't make them the centre of your universe. They will resent you for it eventually and, even worse, they'll grow up with a sense of entitlement that will take decades to undo – if they're lucky.

None of this is rocket science. The only thing that can ruin it is you, or more specifically your ego. Of course you'll both want to fuck other people. Of course you'll get annoyed they've put on a few pounds and don't look quite as pretty/handsome. Of course you'll think it'll be easier with someone new and fresh and exciting. It won't. You'll waste another ten years, end up in exactly the same position, and hate yourself a bit more. Stop it. Realise you can be totally happy with the person you're with right now, get to it, and put all of that 'what if/if only' bullshit energy into other, more constructive things.

The best thing is that all of this can be summed up in two words: be kind. Do not confuse kindness with weakness. Kindness is a dying art. It is the single most important quality in this world and one which is sorely lacking.

When all else fails, think about what your life would be like without your lover. And not the fantasy of shagging everyone in the whole world, having tons of disposable income, sleeping until whenever you like and shitting with the bathroom door open. The gut-wrenching, lonely, cold reality of day after day without that person. Walk a thousand miles in those shoes and then do it again. Spend a few hours really inside that space and looking at it from every angle. Feel it. And then stop being a dick and get back to the job at hand.

Funnily enough, since I've realised this stuff, I have never, ever been happier in a relationship. Hattie and I share something that I never used to understand but always envied in others. We just fit. I am stronger with her in my life, more open, kinder, more able to deal. I fuck up again and again and then I own it, make it right, try harder, put us first. It is the only way, the best way, the most rewarding way. I see her, she sees me and all is well. I look ahead to a future filled with concerts, filming, travelling, writing, living well and my life would be inconceivable without her in it. The best part is that she really, truly digs me. Bafflingly, she thinks I'm hot, talented and occasionally funny. She gives back to me in ways that are unexpected, delightful, considered and wonderful. She is loyal and messy and weird and a brilliant musician and writer. My version of winning the lottery is she and I holding hands at the bus stop in our seventies, one of those couples who people can't help but smile at.

Bach, 'Goldberg Variations', Aria da capo
Glenn Gould, Piano

Bach began and ended his Goldberg Variations with the same thirty-two-bar aria. Thirty-two, incidentally, being the total number of variations in the whole work. The piece has come full circle and ends where it started with the first and last thirty-two bars note-for-note identical. But of course as we listen we are in a very different place from where we were sixty minutes before (as long as the pianist has done his or her job correctly). Bach has taken us on a journey that we interpret and experience through our own memories, feelings and conditioning. You will respond differently from the way I do, and vice versa. That is the glory of music, especially music as immortal as this.

IT FELT RIGHT TO END this book as we began it, with the aria from the Goldbergs. Because that's the thing about music – we hear a piece of music and feel something. We hear the exact same piece of music at a different time and although the music is unchanged, our response is always slightly different.

My own personal 'Goldberg Variations' began as a 7lb baby screaming my lungs out, and my life so far has consisted of many variations — some of them delightful, some brutal, some hopeful and some soaked through with grief and anger. I lost my childhood but gained a child. I lost a marriage but gained a soulmate. I lost my way but gained a career and a fourth or fifth chance at a life that is second to none.

A few short weeks after proposing to Hattie, we're all sitting in my living room watching my first Channel 4 project, which is where this book started. It is the end of many chapters of my weird little life and the beginning of a new one that I hope will be filled with a little less pain, a little more music, and a lot more kindness.

When I end up performing these variations in the future I'm going to play this final aria slower, calmer, more gently than the opening one because at last, that's where my head is at after experiencing this journey variation by variation.

Thank fuck for that.

Afterword

I'VE NO IDEA IF I'M going to survive the next few years. I've been in places before where I felt solid, reliable, good, strong and it's all gone to shit. Sadly I am only ever two bad weeks away from a locked ward.

I've no idea if the thoughts in this book about myself and about music are going to flourish and grow and evolve into something long-lasting and worthwhile.

But I have a strong sense that there is some kind of revolution happening, personally and professionally.

The revolution within me has involved re-evaluating everything I thought I knew and being open to ideas that previously seemed alien, false and impossible. It's taken a long time and come with a huge, barely affordable price tag attached to it.

The revolution outside myself, in the industry that I am devoting my life to, is in its infancy. And I am lucky enough to play a small part in fighting alongside a few others who share the same goals of freeing music from the tyranny of the asshole.

You can help by simply listening to it. Maybe sharing it with a friend. Or sharing it with your kids. It's an honourable thing to do. A kind thing.

Music can shine a light into places where nothing else can reach. That great musical genius lunatic Schumann tells us 'To send light into the darkness of men's hearts – such is the duty of the artist'. I think it's the duty of all of us, no matter what we do to fill our time.

And as long as I'm honouring that, then even if I don't make it I will fall asleep happy.

Acknowledgments

THERE ARE SO MANY PEOPLE without whom I know, for sure, I would not be here. They have been part of my life sometimes for a few hours or days, sometimes for many years. Some are threads that have been part of the entire fabric of my existence, either from the beginning or from the middle. My experience is that as I work through my own shit, I focus on my part, where I'm going wrong, where I can improve, where I can grow up, and then there is a ripple effect. So many of my relationships, both old and new, have blossomed and grown into something I could never have imagined a few years ago. The truth is that as I grow, so do my relationships.

I have chosen a job (or perhaps it has chosen me) that involves the scary and risky reality of spending countless hours alone in a small room or on a big stage, focusing, thinking and feeling. Most of these things are not good for someone with a bit of a wonky head and a bunch of weird and wonderful neuroses. It is by turns safe, terrifying, pressurised and restorative. Sometimes, oddly, all at once.

And amongst all of the people I am surrounded by, there is a small, core group that binds me together and continues to keep me safe and feeling whole.

My mum, who has not once turned her back on me, not once failed to be there in any way she can when I've asked her, who continues to support and encourage and love.

My best friend, best man, best everything, Matthew, whose wife has sewn me up, who has driven me back to hospital more than once, liaised with police and doctors, looked after my ex-wife and son, shouldered burdens and responsibilities that no one should have to shoulder and done it without complaint, with grace, with love.

Sir David Tang, who has subsidised, supported, aided and abetted me in my journey in ways that I could never begin to adequately describe while doing him justice. He is the most generous man I know, and one of the most admirable.

Benedict Cumberbatch, enemy of spellcheckers everywhere, who has offered advice, friendship, movies, dinners, premieres, company, dubious fashion advice, time and energy, many times while in the middle of shooting yet another $100 million dollar epic bloody Hollywood movie. When I knew him at school he was little, bookish, a bit nerdy, quiet, softly spoken and kind. He still is, except for the little part. He is a giant amongst men and the most talented actor of his generation.

Billy Shanahan is my long-suffering and patient psychiatrist. When I first met him (the last in a too-long line of doctors) it was clear I could trust him because he knew what I knew – that life is temporary and indescribably fragile and that there are many, many, too fucking many people for whom suicide is a valid way out. He's that rare breed of doctor who seems to have genuine empathy and understanding, and those two assets are worth a million Xanax.

Derren Brown is, without sounding too creepy, the most genuinely likeable person I have ever met. He has been there for me both personally and professionally for many years now. He is giant of heart, overwhelmingly, frighteningly kind, supportive and absolutely reliable in every way. Should I ever manage to get to a vaguely comparable place in my career to his, I could only ever hope to be a fraction as real and humble as he is. He inspires me more than I can say.

Stephen Fry is not only officiating at our wedding, he is and always has been a staunch supporter of good. He continually sticks his neck out over topics that are uncomfortable, misunderstood, complex and important. He is one of the very few people I know who is exactly the same over a cup of tea at his house as he is in front of the camera talking about manic depression or homosexual injustice. His kindness, advice, support and stupidly big brain have frequently stopped my wobbles from becoming full-on implosions. He is a fucking legend and the only man I would turn for.

My publishers Canongate, with whom I was hit with the threat of legal action over this book in March 2014. Despite doing everything in our power to resolve this amicably, we ended up being forced to go to court in order to fight for the right to publish *Instrumental*. I will always be grateful to Canongate for standing beside me during the fourteen months of aggressive litigation that ensued. It has taken more than anyone could possibly imagine to stay the course, but I am very pleased that the book you have read has not been censored by the British courts in any way.

Denis Blais. You have taken me from being a nobody to being a slightly better known nobody with a bunch of concerts, five albums, TV shows, a tonne of press, a book, DVD, world tours and a happy bank manager. You have done it cautiously, sensibly, carefully and caringly. You have done it when I've pushed, pulled, cried, shouted, screamed and complained. You have not once let me down. You have been responsible for everything that is good in my career and everything that is worthy in my personal life. You are a manager, lawyer, agent, shrink, nurse, bodyguard, photographer, cinematographer, writer, banker, chef, guide, priest, cleaner, consultant, producer, friend, comrade and surrogate father. On we go, together, playing our part in what we set out to do five years ago.

Jack. My boy. You always have been, always will be, the greatest part of my life. One day perhaps you'll be a dad yourself and then you will understand. Until that day comes I can only swear to you, on everything I hold dear, that there is nothing that could come even close to the love and pride I have for you. You're my little cub, the tiny thing I held and fed and cuddled who has grown and explored and become his own, magnificent person. You will always have me, always have a home to come to, never have to worry about doing something you hate simply to pay the mortgage. I want you to do anything and everything that fulfils you and makes you smile. Be whoever you want, and know that I could not be any prouder of who you are. You, more than anyone else in my life, inspire me the most. You are my absolute joy.

And finally Hattie. It is a truth I have only recently discovered, but I now know that the love of a good woman can rescue a man.

And you are so much more than a good woman. You are brave and open and headstrong and vivacious. You have an energy about you that turns my world and my heart upside down and spins it on its axis. For all your delicious quirkiness, there is an all-consuming beauty that radiates from every pore, every cell, in you. And I hope I never, ever get to believe how lucky I am to have you by my side. I want always to feel like I'm falling ever so slightly short and therefore to keep trying harder. I want continually to earn the privilege that is being your man, to show you that my commitment to you, to us, is my immoveable priority. Because I love you. Oh how I fucking love you.

Once there was a fragile man. And he met a fragile woman. They were lucky enough to realise that two fragiles equalled a strong, and so those two little weirdos got married. Because that is unquestionably, truthfully, honestly and absolutely the right thing to do. And one day they went on to have their own weird little cubs. And fucked them up royally like all parents do.

Appendix

'Outrage at Jimmy Savile conceals the fact that our culture encourages paedophilia. Believe me, I know what I'm talking about'

Daily Telegraph **Culture Blog, 1 November 2012**

WE READ MORE AND MORE about the horrors that went on and the now incontestable fact that others knew it was happening, and we get all shouty and indignant. It reveals the irksome, irritating side of Twitter, the tabloid press, self-published blogs and the loud, chatty guy in the pub. The moral high ground. The furious bleating and self-righteousness of the whiter-than-white populace.

The outcry will not do any good at all. How many times since 'Never again' has it happened again? Using words like 'molest' and 'abuse' runs utterly counter to the horror of child rape. As do the prison sentences handed down upon conviction. You can serve longer in prison for saying 'I'm going to kill you' (maximum sentence 10 years) than you can for having sex with your three-year-old daughter (maximum sentence seven years). Newspapers happily show pictures of fourteen-year-old girls sunbathing and use sexual language to describe them while at the same time appearing indignant and appalled at the crimes of Savile, Glitter et al.

The culture of celebrity has the same shroud of secrecy, power and authority as the Church. Why on earth should we be surprised at sexual abuse going on in those circles? The only thing that surprises me is that people actually seem surprised. In any environment where there is power, there will be an abuse of that power.

For five years I was abused at school, at least one other teacher knew it was happening and even after voicing their concerns to the relevant authorities within the school, nothing was done and the horrors continued.

We read about things like this and we think 'how awful' and then get on with eating our cornflakes, but no one really wants to look beneath the surface. The physical act of rape is just the beginning – each time it happened I seemed to leave a little bit of myself behind with him until it felt like there was pretty much nothing left of me that was real. And those bits do not seem to come back over time. What goes too often unreported and unexamined and unacknowledged is the legacy that is left with the victim.

I've talked about this a lot. But some of it bears repeating. Until it's heard by as many people as is necessary to work harder to stop it.

Those side-effects I wrote about earlier: Self-harm. Depression. Drug and alcohol abuse. Reparative surgery. OCD. Dissociation. Inability to maintain functional relationships. Marital breakdowns. Being forcefully institutionalised. Hallucinations (auditory and visual). Hypervigilance. PTSD. Sexual shame and confusion. Anorexia and other eating disorders. These are just a few of my symptoms (for want of a better word) of chronic sexual abuse. They have all been a part of my life in the very recent past, some are still with me, and the abuse I went through was 30 years ago. I am not saying that these things are the inevitable result of my experience; I imagine that some people can go through similar experiences and emerge largely unscathed. What I am saying is that if living life is the equivalent of running a marathon, then sexual abuse in childhood has the net effect of removing one of your legs and adding a backpack of bricks on the starting line.

I don't want to be writing about things like this. I don't want to deal with the inevitable feelings of shame and exposure that will come from it. And I don't want to deal with the accusations of using my back story to flog albums, being full of self-pity, attention-seeking or whatever other madness has already and will no doubt continue being levelled at me. But neither do I want to have to keep quiet, or even worse, feel as if I should keep quiet, when there is so much about our culture (which is in many ways so incredibly evolved) that allows, endorses, encourages and revels in the sexual abuse of children. Paedophilia has acquired a grim, vaguely titillating, car-crash fascination that the press have jumped all over.

We simply cannot on the one hand have sexualised images of children on billboards and magazines, underwear for six-year-olds with pictures of cherries on them, 'school disco' themed nights at bars and community service sentences for downloading 'indecent' images (indecent? Saying 'shit' in church is indecent – this is abominable), and on the other hand regard the Savile story with abject horror. It just does not equate. This is not about censoring what the press can write (typical example from one tabloid: 'She's still only 15, but Chloë Moretz . . . The strawberry blonde stepped out with a male friend in a cute Fifties-style powder blue sleeveless collared shirt which she tied at her waist

– revealing just a hint of her midriff'), or what pictures they can publish. It is about protecting minors who do not have a voice, who are not capable of understanding certain matters and who cannot protect themselves.

This has all been said before. And nothing has really changed. We forget (who would want to remember this stuff?), we think shouting loudly will absolve our collective guilt and change things for the better, we point fingers and form lynch mobs. We paint 'paedo scum' on convicted (or suspected) paedophiles' homes. And yet what we need to do is open our eyes fully and simply not tolerate this, rather like we've done and continue to do so effectively with homophobia and racism. We need to look at providing more visible therapy for both victims, perpetrators and those who have urges that threaten to make them perpetrators. We need to overhaul sentencing guidelines and start tackling the issues with more clarity and integrity. Whatever it takes for as long as it takes needs to be the guiding principle here, because otherwise we will, to use a well-worn but apposite phrase, simply continue the cycle of abuse.

'At last: the Classic BRIT Awards exposed as a sickening crime against classical music'

Daily Telegraph Culture Blog, 8 October 2012

PAUL MORLEY DESERVES A MEDAL. One of the greatest music writers ever, Morley has in one fell swoop exposed the Classic BRIT Awards for what they really are – an offensive, unnecessary, manipulative and dangerous sham.

Sitting there last week at the Royal Albert Hall as a guest of Sinfini (the new classical music website funded, somewhat ironically, by Universal), he describes the horror show that unfurls before him. Morley says what so many of us in the classical world have long thought: 'For those who have come to music through pop or rock, the way "classical music" was dressed up in candelabra kitsch and shop-worn corn would not have persuaded them that there was anything here for them.'

He goes on to discuss the tricks employed by the organisers to deflect the sort of critical perspective that might question its motives, and indeed its tenuous relationship to classical music, or to any music at all.

The key phrase here is 'any music at all'. The people behind the CBAs (an assorted cabal of radio bosses, label heads, PR pundits, agents, promoters, journalists) have, for many years now, diluted and butchered classical music, throwing it into a blender alongside cross-over schmaltz, movie soundtracks, pop-opera and greed, and tried to convince us that the gloopy, sick-making result is 'classical music'.

I urge you I urge you to track down Morley's blog, to read and reread it, print out, laminate and send to the head of every company associated with the bile-inducing cesspit that is the Classic Brit Awards together with a card asking WHAT ARE YOU DOING?

I applaud Sinfini for having the guts to commission that piece — and it is surely no accident that they asked a rock journalist to do it. Most classical pundits would be too terrified to stick their heads above the parapet, given how small the industry is and the knowledge that they would most likely be blacklisted should they come out and criticise the CBAs.

I have wanted to write a piece along these lines for a long time now, but figured (or at least my manager did) it would have made me too easy a target for accusations of jealousy and bitterness, what with me being a concert pianist and therefore, one would think, hungry for a BRIT nomination myself. I was invited to attend this year and my response was that I would rather sh*t in my hands and clap than sit through that. I, naively, went four years ago and vowed never to do so again. Truth be told, I still suffer occasional PTSD-like flashbacks from the experience. I have so far kept my opinions largely to myself but Morley has, gloriously, inspired me to put my cards on the table as well.

The awards were inaugurated by the BPI, and voting is done by 'an academy of industry executives, the media, the British Association of Record Dealers (BARD), members of the Musicians' Union, lawyers, promoters, and orchestra leaders', except for 'Album of the Year' which is voted for by listeners of Classic FM. How did any of these people decide that, in 2011, it was in the best interest of classical music to award Il Divo (the crossover 'opera' quartet signed to Simon Cowell's label) 'artist of the decade'? *Decade.* The most phenomenal classical artist of the LAST TEN YEARS is an operatic pop vocal group created, signed and managed by Cowell! Not Claudio Abbado, Martha Argerich, Stephen Hough, Gustavo Dudamel, Sir Simon Rattle or any one of a thousand internationally acclaimed core classical musicians who have trained, sweated, worked, honed, polished, refined and slaved hours a day for decades to raise their talent to the level necessary to play at Salzburg, Verbier, the Proms, Carnegie Hall. No. A photoshopped, shiny-toothed, suntanned, faux-classical Frankenstein.

Who are these people to purposefully try and convince the general public that Katherine Jenkins is a proper opera singer, that Russell Watson really could handle a week at Covent Garden, that Ludovico Einaudi belongs to the same world as Benjamin Britten, that André Rieu, Andrew Lloyd Webber and Andrea Bocelli are amongst the greatest classical musicians alive today? When did MasterCard give themselves the go-ahead to, year on year, sponsor a conglomerate of people who are force-feeding the musical equivalent of KFC down our throats?

I would, with a bucket of Xanax and an obliging shrink, be able to let this go if I felt it were a case simply of naivety on behalf of the organisers, or indeed even of good intention. But this is not the case. Instead, I am convinced that what we have here is a purposeful, well thought-out, structured plan to chip away year on year, track by track, album by album at the general public, convincing them over time that classical music really does not distinguish Russell Watson from Caruso. That Howard Shore and Beethoven can be mentioned happily in the same awed breath. That Mylene Klass and Vladimir Horowitz are both pianists.

It makes me sick to my stomach. I experience a rage that threatens to overwhelm me listening to those people bleating on about the problems in the classical music industry. YOU ARE THE F****** PROBLEM. Classical music always used to be the music of the people. It is cheap (there are some incredible box-set bargains around), accessible (Spotify puts almost infinite amounts of classical music on every computer connected to the internet) and can be overwhelmingly, brilliantly, aggressively life-changing for all who listen to it. *The Phantom of the Opera* (played with gusto at the awards) is not without its charms, but it is clearly no *Figaro*. And when you invite Gary Barlow, Andrew Lloyd Webber and André Rieu up on stage in the same venue where the Proms provide the real thing, and hold them up as classical musicians you not only belittle classical music, but you belittle us. All of us.

I understand that this is your moment to shine. That this is, in your eyes, the only chance you guys have to be close to the real Brit Awards. You get to be on TV (terrestrial TV, albeit at 11 p.m. on a Sunday), you get to walk the red carpet and smile for the paparazzi (who have no clue who you are or what you do), you get to pretend for one solitary, gauche night that you matter. That you are players. But you're not.

It is an undeniable truth that we will still be listening and talking about Bach, Beethoven, Chopin et al in 300 years. Celebrate that. Glory in that. It is magnificent, profound, enlightening and stupendous. Don't cheapen it with your need for self-esteem. Go hate yourself on someone else's time. The rest of us want actual music. Take a long hard look at the Gramophone Awards or the BBC Music Magazine awards, the genuine Oscars and Emmys of classical where bona fide classical musicians are honoured, and see how it should be done.

The truth is that there is simply no need to go down the Classic BRIT route. What you are in effect saying with this monstrous spectacle is that Joe Public is too uncultured, too dense, too stupid to deal with an unedited, beautifully played Chopin mazurka, Mendelssohn concerto or Beethoven sonata. That instead they need to be drip-fed music from the Hovis ad, complete with funky lighting, glitzy staging and music-hall pomp and told that this is classical music. And that mentality is simply unforgivable, all the more so as it is coming from the very people who should be ambassadors for classical music. Instead you continue to bastardise and cheapen it until very soon it will have been eroded beyond recognition. That, despite all of your empty lies about wanting to bring classical music to a wider audience, is the legacy you are leaving us.

'Classical music needs an enema – not awards'
Guardian Culture Blog, 18 September 2013

CLASSICAL MUSIC IS NOT A glamorous industry. The pay is generally shit and almost always requires vigorous chasing. The people behind it are for the most part stuck in the 1930s and constitutionally incapable of connecting in any way with those born after 1960. The industry has been divided into sharks on the one hand (anything for a buck, even if it involves bastardising the music to an unrecognisable degree) and the 'purebloods' on the other – the Aryan race of the music world where this music is reserved for those who are intelligent and rarefied enough to understand it.

Meanwhile, the presentation and pomp behind it is antiquated, offensive, shrouded in self-importance and irrelevant. But, rather than try and change things, like a chubby, entitled, picked-upon child it looks in all the wrong places to boost its self-esteem. Award ceremonies for the classical industry (industry, not listeners) must have sounded such a terrific idea on paper. Sadly, the mutual masturbatory backslapping and sense of 'better than' that is so rife amongst those who claim to enjoy Varèse and Xenakis only serves to provide the perfect means to further separate what is truly important about classical music from what is deemed as oxygen to those behind it.

The Gramophone Awards are a case in point. First and foremost they need to be congratulated, hugely congratulated, for providing a counterpoint to the Classic BRIT awards. I'm not even going to merit the Classic BRITs with column inches other than to say I would rather commit to a career in clown porn than support them, and let you know that this year, alongside Alfie Boe and Katherine Jenkins, Richard Clayderman's album *Romantique* (seriously) is nominated for Album of the Year. And that it includes a *Les Miserables* medley and his own, inimitable transcription of 'You Raise Me Up'. For those wanting to learn about classical music you would be better off sticking spikes in your ears and necking meths.

Back to the Gramophone Awards. I love *Gramophone* magazine. I am a subscriber and inevitably spend at least £50 every month on CDs after reading their recommendations. In much the same way as someone devoted to trains would go nuts at a Hornby store while clutching his (pristine) copy of *Heritage Railway* magazine, I get off on reading about the latest Rachmaninov recording from (yet) another genius Russian pianist. It is *Heat* magazine for socially awkward classical music fans and nothing more. On the scale of worldly importance it ranks somewhere between peanut butter and Andrex moist wipes – it's rather lovely but by no means essential.

Unlike the vile BRITs, the Gramophones honour bona fide core classical musicians – Sir John Eliot Gardiner, Steven Osborne, Antonio Pappano and others all won much-deserved awards this year. This is a great thing. If Osborne, Pappano et al were footballers they would be household names. But they're not. And, for all the ceremony and spiel, this industry is doing less than nothing to give them the status and recognition they deserve. There was no laughter beyond the occasional inside joke, awkwardly scripted, uptight acceptance speeches, not even the merest hint of inclusion for those who exist outside the classical music world. This was yet another awards ceremony about Self. Self-congratulation, self-celebration, self-importance, where music is kept as the property of a few individuals and yet another wall is erected between music and public. You would get more of a buzz watching a House of Commons webcam than watching last night's award ceremony, even if by some miracle it were televised.

The problem with classical music is that the whole industry is so deeply ashamed of itself, so unremittingly apologetic for being involved with an art form seen as irrelevant, privileged and poncey, that it has gone to unfortunate extremes to over-compensate. Classical, as a genre, has become the musical equivalent of cranking (look it up). And if it didn't break my heart quite so much, I'd simply laugh and get back to practising my little upright piano. But the legacy it is leaving us and the price we all will pay for this is too distressing to ignore.

EM Forster wrote that a Beethoven symphony was 'the most sublime noise that has ever penetrated the ear of man'. Goethe called architecture 'frozen music'. Classical music has been around for centuries because it has an unceasing, infallible and soul-shattering ability to take all of us on a journey of self-discovery and improvement in a world where most other means of doing so seem to involve either Simon Cowell or Deepak Chopra. It is a right, not a luxury, and, at the risk of sounding like a haughty middle-class mother at a children's birthday party, the industry behind it is ruining it for the rest of us.

The impotent bleating about reaching younger audiences, the evident pride Classic FM takes in playing a twelve-minute-long piece of music ('our big piece after 6 p.m.'), the endless movie-themed 'classical' shows on radio, the total and utter segregation of classical music on TV, radio and press, the inevitable Halls of Fame, compilation best of box-sets, Tchaikovsky 1812 overtures – with cannon and mortar effects (war veterans stay away) all chip away relentlessly at the underlying fabric of what makes classical music so infinite and great.

Last night, despite an irritatingly brilliant performance from Benjamin Grosvenor (he really is as good as they say) and a Lifetime Achievement acceptance speech that showed Julian Bream to be a total dude and refreshingly human in an otherwise stultifying vacuum, was just more pomp and pointlessness. Universally white (save for the waiting staff), nettle cordial and lamb on the tables for the smartphone-addicted guests, piped classical music (seriously – if the Gramophone Awards are happy to pump it out at barely audible levels then what hope is there?), and the air of ennui so thick you could choke on it.

If our politicians are going to continue to cut arts funding and appear answerable to no one, then surely it is up to the industry itself to stamp its feet and make some changes. Christ, Beethoven was so horrified at the treatment of classical musicians and composers he put an immediate stop to being treated like a servant – he kicked down the doors, planted bombs under his audience's seats and unapologetically claimed his place as the man who heralded in the Romantic age. Today, we spend a few quid getting industry insiders drunk on dodgy wine in a cold, dark room for four long hours.

No matter how much I worship Steven Osborne, Zoltán Kocsis and the other stellar Gramophone Award winners from 2013, nothing, absolutely nothing, has changed for the better in either the perception of classical music or the prognosis for it after last night's ceremony. I wish I'd stayed at home listening to Glenn Gould.

If you have been affected or triggered by any of the issues in my book and need help or advice then please go to NAPAC (**napac.org.uk**), Survivors UK (**survivorsuk.org**) or Mind (**mind.org.uk**) to get support.

napac   SURVIVORSUK   mind

CANON▌▌GATE.tV

CHANNELLING GREAT CONTENT

WATCH

INTERVIEWS, TRAILERS, ANIMATIONS, READINGS, GIGS

LISTEN

AUDIO BOOKS, PODCASTS, MUSIC, PLAYLISTS

READ

CHAPTERS, EXCERPTS, SNEAK PEEKS, RECOMMENDATIONS

DISCOVER

BLOGS, EVENTS, NEWS, CREATIVE PARTNERS

SHOP

LIMITED EDITIONS, BUNDLES, SECRET SALES